Reach
HIGHER

Program Authors

Nancy Frey

Lada Kratky

Nonie K. Lesaux

Sylvia Linan-Thompson

Deborah J. Short

Jennifer D. Turner

NATIONAL
GEOGRAPHIC
L E A R N I N G

Australia · Brazil · Mexico · Singapore · United Kingdom · United States

NATIONAL GEOGRAPHIC
L E A R N I N G

National Geographic Learning,
a Cengage Company

Reach Higher 4B
Program Authors: Nancy Frey, Lada Kratky,
Nonie K. Lesaux, Sylvia Linan-Thompson,
Deborah J. Short, Jennifer D. Turner

Publisher, Content-based English:
  Erik Gundersen

Associate Director, R&D: Barnaby Pelter

Senior Development Editors:
  Jacqueline Eu

  Ranjini Fonseka

  Kelsey Zhang

Director of Global Marketing: Ian Martin

Heads of Regional Marketing:
  Charlotte Ellis (Europe, Middle East and Africa)

  Kiel Hamm (Asia)

  Irina Pereyra (Latin America)

Product Marketing Manager: David Spain

Senior Production Controller: Tan Jin Hock

Senior Media Researcher (Covers): Leila Hishmeh

Senior Designer: Lisa Trager

Director, Operations: Jason Seigel

Operations Support:
  Rebecca Barbush

  Drew Robertson

  Caroline Stephenson

  Nicholas Yeaton

Manufacturing Planner: Mary Beth Hennebury

Publishing Consultancy and Composition:
  MPS North America LLC

ISBN-13: 978-0-357-36695-0

National Geographic Learning
200 Pier Four Blvd
Boston, MA 02210
USA

Locate your local office at **international.cengage.com/region**

Visit National Geographic Learning online at **ELTNGL.com**
Visit our corporate website at **www.cengage.com**

Printed in Mexico
Print Number: 03 Print Year: 2022

Contents at a Glance

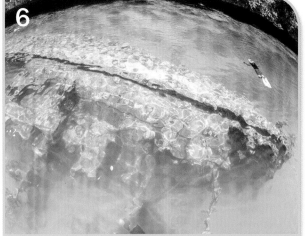

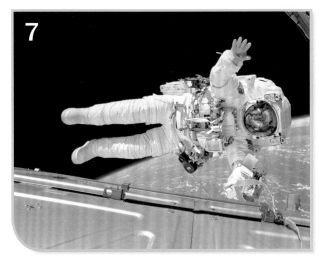

Table of Contents

Invaders!

Unit 5

Table of Contents

Treasure Hunters

Unit 6

Table of Contents

Moving Through Space

Unit 7

(?) BIG QUESTION

What does it take to explore space?

SCIENCE
▸ Solving Problems
▸ Speed
▸ Space

Table of Contents

Saving a Piece of the World

Unit 8

Genres at a Glance

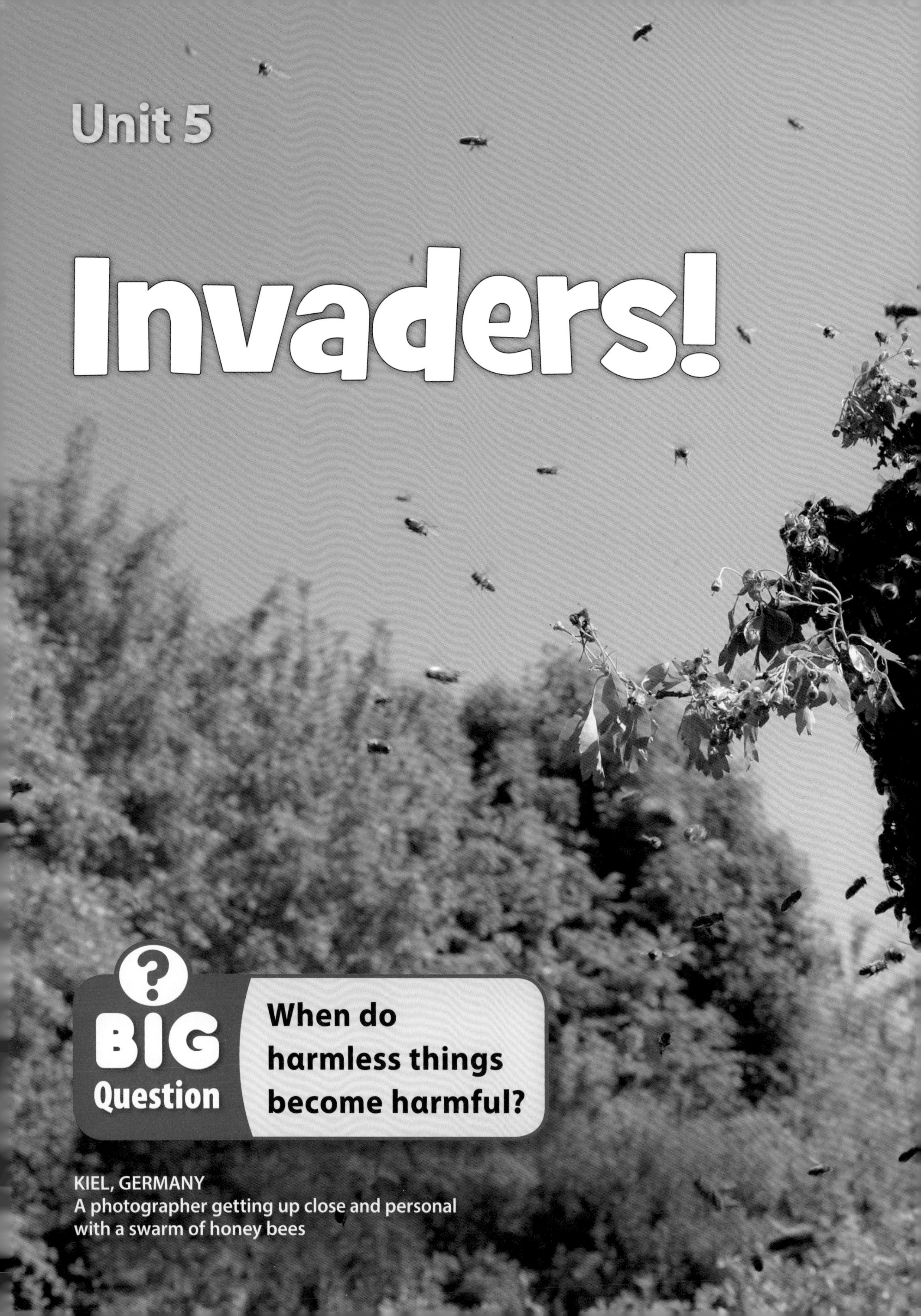

Invaders!

?
BIG
Question

When do harmless things become harmful?

KIEL, GERMANY
A photographer getting up close and personal
with a swarm of honey bees

Unit at a Glance
▸ **Language Focus**: Retell a Story, Define and Explain
▸ **Reading Strategy**: Make Inferences
▸ **Topic**: Ecosystems

Share What You Know

Do It!

❶ **Think** of a time when you really noticed something in nature. This thing might have surprised you.

❷ **Draw** a picture of what you saw.

❸ **Tell** the class about what made you notice this thing in nature. What was different about it?

Retell a Story

Listen to Diego's song. Then listen as he retells the story. Tell your partner a story about weeds in your neighborhood. Listen to your partner's story. Use **Language Frames** as you retell each other's stories.

Song 🔊 ♪

Flowers or Weeds?

When Johnny dropped sunflower seeds in the park,

Sprouts grew and grew.

When Johnny dropped sunflower seeds in the park,

Sprouts grew and grew.

They grew on the trails and they grew on the lawn,

By the end of the summer the grass was all gone.

And we all were sorry that Johnny had dropped those seeds.

Tune: "When Johnny Comes Marching Home"

Before Johnny arrived, the park had a beautiful lawn.

Key Words

decompose

experiment

humid

mold

spore

🔊 Key Words

Look at the picture. Use **Key Words** and other words to talk about a science **experiment** with food.

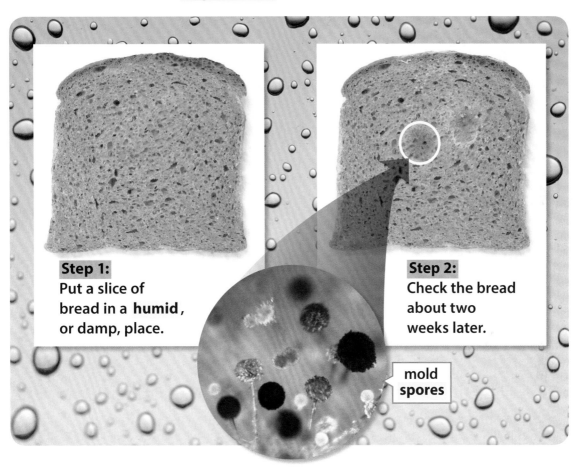

Step 1:
Put a slice of bread in a **humid**, or damp, place.

Step 2:
Check the bread about two weeks later.

mold spores

In this science experiment, **mold** grows on bread and **decomposes** it.

Talk Together

Make up a story about mold. Use **Language Frames** from page 4 and **Key Words** in your story. Tell it to a partner. Then have your partner retell the story and explain if the mold was harmful or harmless.

Plot

The events in a story go together to form the story's **plot**. The events follow a certain order, or sequence. You can summarize the plot. First, think about the most important things that happen. Then, tell these events in sequence.

Look at these pictures of Diego's vine.

Map and Talk

You can use an events chain to summarize the plot. In the first box, write about the first important event. In the next box, write about the next event. Keep writing the most important events in sequence.

Events Chain

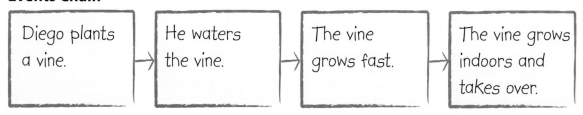

| Diego plants a vine. | → | He waters the vine. | → | The vine grows fast. | → | The vine grows indoors and takes over. |

Listen as your partner tells a story about a fast-growing plant. Make an events chain to summarize the events of the story.

🔊 More Key Words

Use these words to talk about "The Fungus That Ate My School" and "Mold Terrarium."

contain
verb

To **contain** something is to hold it inside. This jar **contains** many coins.

control
verb

To **control** something is to be in charge of it. The driver **controls** where the car goes.

environment
noun

An **environment** is the area where something lives. Plants grow well in a sunny **environment**.

investigate
verb

When you **investigate** something, you find out about it. The boy **investigates** the cave.

spread
verb

To **spread** is to cover a wider area. Flies can **spread** diseases.

Talk Together

Work with a partner. Make a Word Web for each **Key Word**.

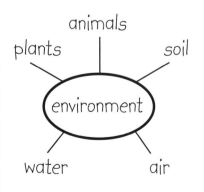

animals
plants
soil
environment
water
air

7

Learn to Make Inferences

Look at the picture. Diego does not say what he forgot to do. Look for clues to figure out, or **make an inference** about, what he forgot.

You can **make inferences** when you read, too.

How to Make Inferences

1. Look for details in the text.

2. Think about what you already know about the details and the topic.

3. Put your ideas together. What else can you figure out about the details?

I read _____.

I know _____.

And so _____.

Talk Together

Read Diego's retelling of a fairy tale. Read the sample inference. Then use **Language Frames** to tell a partner about the inferences you made while reading.

Fairy Tale

Jack and the Beanstalk

Jack went to buy some food. He met a man on the road.

"Buy my SUPER SEEDS," cried the man. "It's true! In just a week, you can feed your whole family with the food from just one bean seed."

Sample Inference

"I read the man's promises.

I know that plants can't grow that fast.

And so I think the man wants to trick Jack."

Jack bought the dried seeds and planted them in his backyard. It was a perfect **environment** for growing beans.

In just a few days, the plant had **spread** across the yard. It was out of **control**! The garden wasn't big enough to **contain** the huge stalk, which began to climb high into the sky.

Jack decided to **investigate**. So he climbed the plant lightly, careful not to crush the stalk. Finally, he reached a cloud. There, he found a box filled with bright, shiny gold. Jack grabbed the gold and climbed quickly down the stalk.

Then Jack heard a rumble in the sky. The beanstalk started to shake. ◀

Jack took an axe and chopped down the stalk. He heard someone shouting in the clouds. Jack sighed with relief. Then he used the gold to buy some real food for his family. ◀

◀ = A good place to make an inference

Read a Story

Genre

Most **science fiction** stories are based on ideas in science. Even if the events seem realistic, they probably could not really happen.

Narrator's Point of View

The person who tells a story is the narrator. If the narrator is one of the characters, then the story uses the first-person point of view. First-person narrators use the words *we* and *I*.

A first-person narrator uses the words *we* and *I*.

We told Mr. Harrison our science experiments were **getting out of control**.

The Fungus That Ate My School

by **Arthur Dorros** • illustrated by **David Catrow**

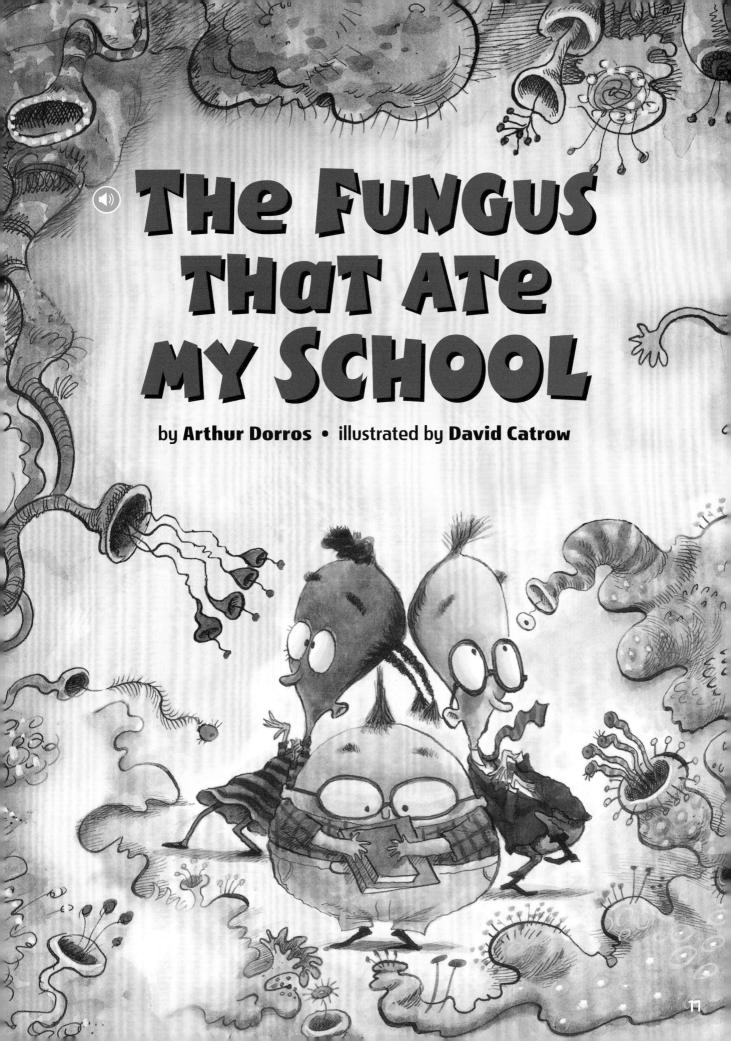

▶ **Set a Purpose**
Find out what happens with a science
experiment during spring vacation.

We told Mr. Harrison our science
experiments were **getting out of control** .

He didn't believe us, until **IT** ate our school.

IT started before spring vacation. Our class was
studying fungus. We were growing fungus in jars.

"Are you sure our experiments will be all right
while we're not here?" we asked Mr. Harrison.

"Don't worry," he told us, "fungus can take care
of itself."

Mr. Harrison

getting out of control growing too fast

Ms. Moreover

There was rain during the whole vacation. Our first day back at school, Ms. Moreover, the principal, opened the front doors early.

"Come on, children, let's get out of the rain."

We walked into the dark hallway. Ms. Moreover turned on the lights.

"AAAG!" yelled Ellen.

Green, yellow, and purple **fuzz** covered everything.

"What is **IT**?" asked Ms. Moreover.

"**IT**'s big and ugly," said Ellen.

"**IT**'s **fantastic**!" I said.

"**IT** is *not* fantastic," said Ms. Moreover.

"That's true, **IT**'s a fungus!" said Mr. Harrison.

fuzz fungus
fantastic amazing; wonderful

▶ **Before You Continue**

1. **Plot** What happens at school during spring vacation?
2. **Point of View** Is this story written in the first person or third person point of view? Explain how you know.

▶ **Predict**
What caused the fungus to grow?

The bell rang. Actually, the bell went *thud, thud, thud.* **IT** had **smothered** the bell. The **slimy** fuzz covered the floors, walls, bulletin boards, even the lights.

"**IT**'s eating everything!" I said.

"I don't hear **IT** chewing," Ellen **noted**.

"I didn't think fungus had a mouth," said Alex.

"Look! **IT**'s eating our **universe**!" cried Ellen.

smothered covered
slimy wet
noted said
universe models of the planets and sun

IT **squished** under our feet as we **tromped** down the damp hallway. Water splattered on our heads.

"The roof's been leaking," Mr. Harrison said.

"That's definitely a problem," said Ms. Moreover. She opened the office door. "IT has taken over my office!"

We **ventured** further through the dark halls. Mr. Page, the librarian, looked into the library.

"Oh, no," said Mr. Page. He fainted.

End of Page.

---

squished made strange sounds
tromped walked
ventured went

▶ **Before You Continue**
1. **Plot** What does Mr. Harrison discover?
2. **Make Inferences** What does the author mean by "End of Page?"

15

▶ **Predict**
How will Mr. Harrison solve the
problem of the fungus?

Mr. Harrison let us into our classroom.

"**IT** ate my notebook!" cried Alex.

"**IT**'s eating my homework!" cried Ellen.

"Just as I thought," said Ms. Moreover when she saw the jars of fungus we'd been growing. "**IT** must be one of your class's **experiments**."

"**IT** doesn't look like mine," I said.

"We need **an expert opinion**," said Mr. Harrison. "I know just who to call."

an expert opinion help from someone
who knows about fungus

Professor Macademia

We went to the cafeteria.

"Don't let **IT** eat the food!" said Ms. Moreover. Too late.

"Looks like **IT** can eat almost anything," I said.

"Quickly, children, run!" said Ms. Moreover, "I mean *walk* to the nearest **exit**."

A car pulled up.

"Professor Macademia is here," Mr. Harrison said, "she knows fungus."

"She looks like she knows fungus," said Ellen.

"Amazing," said Professor Macademia, "**IT**'s **a jewel, a treasure**!"

"How can we get rid of **IT**?" Ms. Moreover asked. "That's all I want to know."

exit way out
a jewel, a treasure very special

The Fungus Unit

"Fresh air, light, **elbow grease**, and a little help from my friends in the Fungus Unit ought to **get rid of IT**," said Professor Macademia.

"Fungus Unit? What's a Fungus Unit?" Ellen asked.

"Special **branch** of the Sanitation Department," said someone dressed in white, pulling a giant hose into the school. Other workers carried in shovels, mops, and big lights.

"Action!" called one of them.

Suddenly the whole school was filled with whirring and clanking, swooshing and scrubbing.

elbow grease hard work
get rid of IT clean up the fungus
branch part

The Fungus Unit **scraped IT** off of
everything in the school and **hauled IT** away.
Professor Macademia kept our fungus
experiments. "I want to see if one of them is **IT**,"
she said. She held up one of the fungus jars. "Aha!"
said Professor Macademia. "This is **IT**!"

"It's not mine," said Alex.

"Uh-oh," I said, "**IT**'s mine."

scraped cleaned
hauled took

▶ **Before You Continue**

1. **Plot** Who does Mr. Harrison call?
   How do they clean up the fungus?
2. **Make Inferences** What does the narrator
   mean by "Uh-oh...IT's mine?"

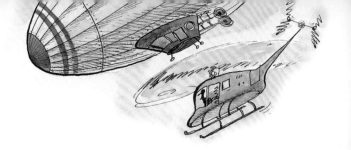

▶ **Predict**
What will happen to the students
who grew the fungus?

"It's not your fault," said Professor Macademia.
"The wet, closed-up school was the perfect place for a fungus to
grow. You have made a great discovery! This fungus belongs in
the Museum of Fungus and Industry!"

Our class got a special award from the museum.

"Congratulations, class," Ms. Moreover said. "However,
Mr. Harrison, I think you've learned enough about fungus for now."

"Don't worry," said Mr. Harrison. "No more fungus
experiments—until next year." ❖

OUR
Golden
Moldy

▶ **Before You Continue**
1. **Confirm Prediction** Do any students get in
   trouble? Why or why not?
2. **Plot** Why does the class get an award?

Meet the Author

Arthur Dorros

Why did Arthur Dorros write about a fungus that *eats* a school? It might be because he lives in the Pacific Northwest of the United States, a damp region where fungus grows easily. "A fungus got my shoe, another started eating its way through my clothes, and there's a fungus in our basement," he says.

Many of Mr. Dorros's book ideas come from things that happened to him. When he was four years old, his parents took him to an alligator farm. They thought it would be nice to take a picture of Arthur and the alligators. They didn't worry that there wasn't a fence between Arthur and the alligators. Fortunately, the alligators didn't *eat* Arthur! That experience later inspired his book *Alligator Shoes*.

▲ Arthur Dorros, as a child, at the alligator farm

Writing Tip ✏️

Write a brief paragraph about the similarities between Arthur Dorros's life and the characters and events in this story. Then write about the characters and events that are probably different from anything that could happen in the author's life.

Key Words	
contain	humid
control	investigate
decompose	mold
environment	spore
experiment	spread

Talk About It

1. How do you know that the story is **science fiction**?

The story is science fiction because _____ .

2. Imagine that you are one of the workers in the Fungus Unit. **Retell the story** of the science **experiment** from your point of view.

Before we arrived, _____ . During spring vacation, _____ .

3. What do the characters in the story think about the fungus? Name two characters. Contrast their opinions of the fungus.

_____ likes the fungus because _____ .

_____ does not like the fungus because _____ .

Write About It

What do you think will happen in Mr. Harrison's science class next year? Write two paragraphs to continue the story. First, write some ideas. Use **Key Words** as you plan your writing. Then organize your ideas as you write your draft.

Another year passed by. Mr. Harrison wondered _____ .

Plot

Make an events chain to summarize the plot of "The Fungus That Ate My School." Tell the events in sequence. Notice how some events influence what happens later in the plot.

Events Chain

| The students study fungus. | → | They leave for vacation. | → | | → |

Write the first important event.   **Write the next important event.**

Now use your events chain as you retell the story to a partner. Use as many **Key Words** as you can. Record your retelling.

First, _____ .
Next, _____ .
Then, _____ .

Fluency

Practice reading with expression.
Rate your reading.

How is fungus both harmless and harmful? Working in a group, make two lists. Use **Key Words** in your lists.

Antonyms

Antonyms are words with opposite meanings. Writers use them to show contrast: This morning fungus covered **everything**. By noon, **nothing** had any fungus on it.

Sometimes a word like *not* or *but* signals the use of antonyms: The fungus seemed **ordinary**, <u>but</u> I knew it was **special**.

You might see antonyms on tests in **word analogies**. An analogy shows how two words relate to each other.

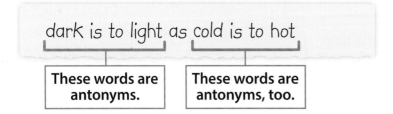

dark is to light as cold is to hot

| These words are antonyms. | These words are antonyms, too. |

The relationship between both pairs of words is the same. They are opposites.

Try It Together

Read each item. Choose the word that best completes the analogy.

1. **Fantastic is to terrible as special is to** _____.
   A super
   B nasty
   C unique
   D ordinary

2. **Treasure is to trash as expert is to** _____.
   A professional
   B beginner
   C silly
   D unknown

Making Connections In this science **experiment**, you'll **investigate** how fungus grows.

Genre A **science experiment** helps test an idea. It has a list of materials and a list of steps to follow. Sometimes the text explains the results, too.

Mold Terrarium

from *The Science Explorer*

Materials List

leftover bread, fruit, vegetables, or cheese, cut into small pieces

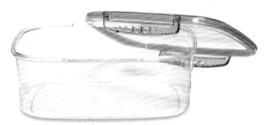

clear plastic container with a lid

water

tape

▶ **Before You Continue**

1. **Make Connections** Based on what you know about **mold**, why do you think you need water to do the **experiment**?

2. **Use Text Features** Look at the photos. What do they show you?

25

Steps to Follow

1 Dip each piece of food into some water and put it into your container. Try to **spread** the pieces out so they are close to each other but not all in a **heap**.

2 Put the lid on the container. Put tape around the edge of the lid to **seal it**.

3 Put the container in a place where no one will **knock it over** or throw it away.

heap pile
seal it make sure no
    air can get in or out
knock it over spill it

4 Every day, look at the food in your **terrarium**. Do not open the container. After two or three days, you should see blue or green or white **fuzzy stuff** growing on some of the pieces of food. After a few more days, some of the food may start to **rot**. For about two weeks, you can watch how the **mold spreads** and how things rot. After that, it'll get boring, because not much more will happen.

mold

▲ After two or three days, mold will start to appear.

terrarium container
fuzzy stuff mold
rot decompose

▶ **Before You Continue**

1. **Steps in a Process** What might happen if you did not perform step 2 of the **experiment**? Explain.

2. **Use Text Features** Look at the photo on this page. What information does it show? Explain.

Here are some things to notice:

- Which food started getting moldy first?

- What color is the **mold**?

- What texture is the mold? Is it flat, fuzzy, or bumpy?

- Does mold **spread** from one piece of food to another?

- Do different kinds of mold grow on different types of food?

⚠️ DANGER!

When you're through with your mold terrarium, throw it in the garbage. Don't reuse the container. Don't even open the lid! Mold is not good for people to smell or breathe in.

through finished

What is mold, anyway?

That fuzzy stuff growing on the food is **mold**, a kind of fungus. Mushrooms are one kind of fungus. Molds are another.

Unlike plants, molds don't grow from seeds. They grow from tiny **spores** that float in the air. When spores fall onto a piece of damp food, they often grow into mold.

Green plants are green because they **contain** a chemical called chlorophyll. Chlorophyll allows green plants to capture the sun's energy and use it to make food from air and water. Unlike green plants, mold and other fungi have no chlorophyll and can't make their own food.

▲ **Brown mushrooms are a kind of fungus.**

▼ **Molds grow from tiny spores like these.**

---

damp slightly wet

▶ **Before You Continue**

1. **Details** Why shouldn't you reuse the plastic container from this **experiment**?
2. **Compare/Contrast** How are **molds** different from plants?

How does mold feed itself?

The **mold** that grows in a mold terrarium feeds on bread, cheese, and other foods. The mold produces chemicals that make the food break down and start to rot. As the bread rots, the mold grows.

How Mold Feeds Itself

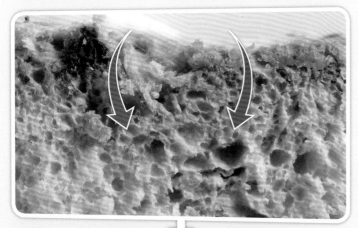

◀ Mold produces chemicals that make the bread start to rot.

◀ The rotting bread releases nutrients that cause the mold to grow.

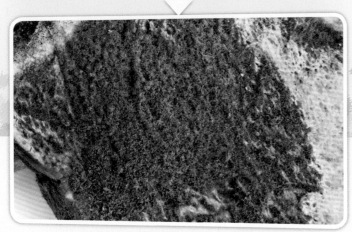

◀ The mold growth **spreads** across the bread.

Who wants this stuff around?

It can be annoying to find moldy food in your refrigerator. In nature, though, **mold** is very useful. It helps break down dead plants and animals. In a natural **environment**, rotting things return to the soil, providing nutrients for other plants. Mold is a natural recycler. ❖

▼ Mold is an important part of the natural **environment**.

▶ **Before You Continue**

1. **Make Inferences** What might happen in a forest if there were no **mold**?
2. **Use Text Features** Look at the diagram on page 30. Explain what it shows.

Key Words

contain	humid
control	investigate
decompose	mold
environment	spore
experiment	spread

Compare Author's Purpose

Each genre, or form of writing, has a certain purpose. An **author's purpose** for writing science fiction is different from the purpose for writing an **experiment**.

Compare "The Fungus That Ate My School" and "Mold Terrarium." Work with a partner to complete the checklist.

Comparison Chart

Purpose	Science Fiction Story	Science Experiment
Tells about a science idea	✓	
Tests a science idea		✓
Tells how to do something		
Is mostly fun to read		
Describes events that probably can't happen		

Write a checkmark if it has this purpose.

Talk Together

When do living things become harmful? Think about the science fiction story and science experiment you just read. Use **Key Words** to talk about your ideas.

Adjectives

An **adjective** tells about a noun. You can use adjectives to describe things or to compare things.

Grammar Rules Adjectives

• Use adjectives to tell about the color, size, or shape of something.	**Round** blobs of **purple** fuzz covered the **long** walls.
• Use adjectives to tell how something sounds, feels, looks, tastes, or smells.	We heard **loud** sounds. We saw **fluffy** puffs of smoke.
• Some adjectives even tell how something is used.	The **cleaning** fluids had a **horrible** smell.
• Add -**er** to a one-syllable adjective when you compare two things.	The fungus in the library was damp**er** than in the hall.
• Add -**est** to a one-syllable adjective to compare three or more things.	The great**est** experiments can happen by accident.

Read Adjectives

Read these sentences from "The Fungus That Ate My School." What adjectives can you find?

It squished under our feet as we tromped down the damp hallway. We ventured further through the dark halls.

Write Adjectives

What fun experiments have you done? Write a paragraph describing one of them. Try to use adjectives in different ways.

Language Focus

Language Frames

- _____ happened because _____ .
- This is important because _____ .

Define and Explain

Listen to Mona's poem. Then use **Language Frames** to define and explain what is happening in the animals' environment.

Poem

Nowhere to Hide

We are coyotes, foxes, and deer.

We used to live here.

This was our neighborhood. This was our home.

But now there is no room for us.

This happened because people built houses and roads and office parks and malls.

This is important because we have nowhere to hide.

We must find a new home.

We are coyotes, foxes, and deer.

We are not safe here.

🔊 Key Words

Look at the picture. Use **Key Words** and other words to talk about how people affect wildlife.

Key Words
habitat
invade
population
species
threatened

People **invade**, or take over, a **habitat**. The homes for wildlife disappear.

The **population** of this place has always been animals. Where will they go now?

Each animal **species**, or special group, needs a place to live and find food. Without the right habitat, the animals are **threatened**. Their lives are in danger.

Talk Together

How do some species become harmful to others? Talk about this question in a small group. Try to use **Language Frames** from page 34 and **Key Words** as you define and explain.

Problem and Solution

When someone describes a **problem**, what information do you expect to learn? First, you need to know what the problem is. Then, you might need some examples of it. Finally, you want to know about a possible **solution** to the problem.

Look at the pictures of armadillos on the highway.

Map and Talk

You can make a problem-and-solution chart to organize the information you receive about a problem. First, describe the problem. Then write any examples of it. Finally, tell about the solution.

Problem-and-Solution Chart

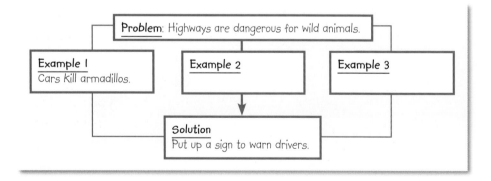

Think of a problem in your neighborhood or environment. Tell a partner about it. Make a problem-and-solution chart together.

◉ More Key Words

Use these words to talk about "Aliens from Earth" and "Island Observations."

balance
noun

When something is in **balance**, it is steady. If the girl keeps her **balance**, she will not fall.

competition
noun

A **competition** is a contest. The runners are in a **competition** to win the race.

introduce
verb

When people **introduce** themselves, they meet for the first time. A handshake is a friendly way to **introduce** yourself.

migration
noun

During a **migration**, people or animals move from one place to another.

native
adjective

When living things are **native** to an area, they live and grow there naturally.

Talk Together

Give clues about a **Key Word** until your partner guesses it correctly. Take turns.

> The last part of this word sounds like **loose**.

Learn to Make Inferences

Look at the picture. What kind of animal does it show? Where does it live? Look at the details to figure out, or **make inferences** about, this animal's natural environment.

You also **make inferences** when you read.

How to Make Inferences

 1. Look for details in the text.

 2. Think about what you already know about the details and the topic.

 3. Put your ideas together. What else can you figure out from the details?

I read _____ .

I know _____ .

And so _____ .

Talk Together

Read this news story about Mona. Read the sample inference. Then use **Language Frames** to tell a partner about the inferences you made while reading.

News Story

Fourth-Grader Rescues Orphan Armadillo

ELGIN, TX—One young armadillo is safe, thanks to local fourth-grader, Mona Nighthorse.

While taking part in a highway clean-up, Ms. Nighthorse found a baby armadillo. The animal's mother was dead on the highway. Ms. Nighthorse called the Animal Care Center. Dr. Jay Abasi told her to bring the orphaned armadillo to the center.

Ms. Nighthorse agreed to help Dr. Abasi care for the baby, which she named *Redonda*.

"At first, we fed her with an eyedropper," explained Ms. Nighthorse. "Later, we had to be careful to balance her diet. We gave her some cat food. But we also fed her things she would find in nature. Redonda loves worms and ants."

Dr. Abasi and Ms. Nighthorse plan to introduce Redonda back into the wild.

"We know she will be happier there," said Ms. Nighthorse. "But she has to be able to survive the **competition** with other animals." ◀

Today, armadillos are **native** to Texas, but they were not always found in Elgin. **Migration** brought the beloved **species** to the area during the 19th century. ◀

Sample Inference

"I read that the animal's mother was dead.

I know that armadillos often get hit by cars.

And so I think the mother was probably hit by a car."

◀ = A good place to make an inference

39

Read a Science Text

Genre
Science texts are nonfiction. They give detailed information about different science topics.

Text Features
The text is divided into sections. The **heading** tells the topic for that section. A **topic sentence** states the main idea about the topic.

heading

What Healthy Ecosystems Need

topic sentence

Aliens are plants or animals that invade another ecosystem, a natural community of plants and animals living in balance with one another. Scientists call these aliens *exotics*, a word that means "to come from outside."

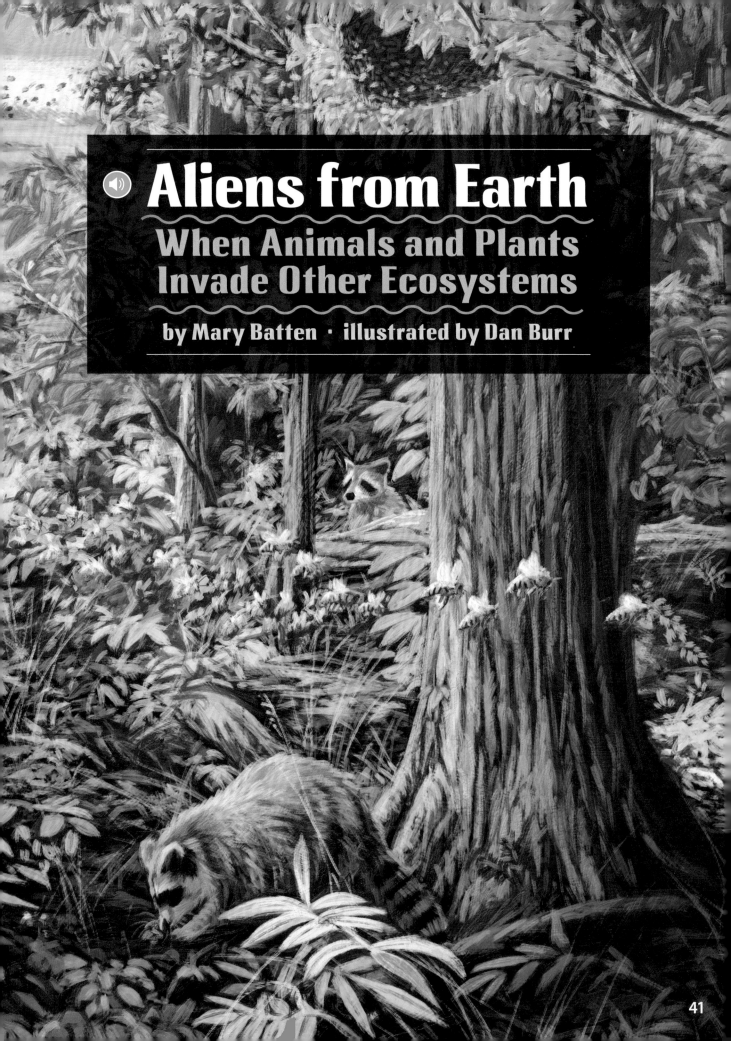

Aliens from Earth

When Animals and Plants Invade Other Ecosystems

by Mary Batten · illustrated by Dan Burr

▸ **Set a Purpose**
Find out what happens when alien
species invade an ecosystem.

Asia

ancient land
bridge

What Healthy Ecosystems Need

Aliens are plants or animals that **invade** another
ecosystem, a natural community of plants and animals
living in **balance** with one another. Scientists call these
aliens *exotics*, a word that means "to come from outside."

A healthy ecosystem needs a variety of **organisms** and a
balance between predators and prey. Alien invaders can
upset the balance of an ecosystem and threaten it.

Pacific Ocean

organisms living things
upset harm

For millions of years, living things traveled from one place to another. Animals walked, flew, and crawled across ancient land bridges from one continent to another. Carried by wind, water, birds, and other animals, seeds moved from place to place.

For most of the planet's history, the movement of plants and animals happened very slowly. Ecosystems stayed in **balance** because they were able to change gradually over time.

North America

▲ An ancient land bridge allowed living things to migrate from Asia to North America.

▶ Before You Continue

1. **Problem/Solution** What is an alien invasion? Why is it considered a problem?

2. **Make Inferences** Why do you think the movement of plants and animals across Earth was slow in the past?

How People Change Ecosystems ~

Humans greatly **sped up the pace** of alien invasions. As human **populations** grew, people needed more natural resources. Eventually they moved into places where human beings had never lived before. They hunted animals, gathered **native** plants, and learned to farm. Wherever people settled, they changed the **habitat**.

Over the centuries, people invented ways to go longer distances and to move around faster. When people began traveling by ship, they took animals such as goats, dogs, cats, and chickens with them. They also took seeds of plants they liked to eat. These **migrations** changed **native** ecosystems more quickly.

Today, every living thing you can imagine—**viruses**, **bacteria**, insects, plants, sea creatures—travels on the same planes and ships that carry people and **cargo**. Invaders move quickly all over the globe. It is becoming harder to **maintain** the delicate **balance** in the world's ecosystems.

sped up the pace increased the speed
viruses, bacteria tiny germs
cargo goods
maintain keep

▶ **Before You Continue**

1. **Use Text Features** Read the heading and the first sentence on page 44. What is the topic of this section?
2. **Problem/Solution** What problem was created by human **migration**?

Islands in Danger ~~~

Islands, surrounded by water and **cut off** from other lands, are especially **at risk**. Until recently, few new **species** were able to cross the ocean to reach **distant** islands. Today, any ship or plane that goes to an island could carry an alien invader. Alien invasions can hurt even a large island continent like Australia.

▲ **Ships and planes can carry alien invaders into islands such as Australia.**

cut off separated
at risk threatened
distant far-off

▲ Today rabbits cause serious problems for Australian farmers.

About 200 years ago, Europeans **colonized** the island of Australia. They took rabbits, foxes, and other animals with them. They also took cats to kill the rats that had arrived on settlers' ships. The cats did not **encounter** any predators, so their numbers grew quickly.

Rabbits also had no natural predators, so the rabbit **population** also **exploded**. In 2003, Australia had more than 500 million rabbits. These **pests** destroy soil, damage farmers' crops, and wreck the **habitat** of many **native species**.

colonized settled on
encounter find
exploded grew quickly
pests animals that cause problems

▶ Before You Continue

1. **Use Text Features** What do the heading and topic sentence on page 46 tell you?
2. **Make Inferences** How could the increase in the rabbit **population** have been prevented?

Starlings

You don't have to live on an island to see an alien.
You may find one in your own backyard.

Starlings live throughout the United States, but these
birds are not **native**. In the 1890s, some people in
New York decided to **import** all of the birds mentioned
in the plays of William Shakespeare, a famous writer. They
brought in some starlings along with the other birds. The
people did not realize the problems the starlings might cause.
These **aggressive** birds compete with native birds for food and
take over the nests of some **species**. There are now about
200 million starlings in the United States.

▲ starling

import bring into one country
from another country
aggressive bold and fierce

Killer Bees

In 1956, a scientist brought some African bees to Brazil, a country in South America. Then someone accidentally released the bees from their hive. **Swarms** of bees flew away into the forest.

The scientist thought that the African bees would die in the forest. Instead, they bred with local honeybees. The **offspring** are called Africanized honeybees, or killer bees. These exotic bees defend their hives more fiercely than other honeybees. They have stung to death some farm animals and even a few people.

▼ **Africanized bees**

Swarms Large groups
offspring bees that were born from these parents

▶ **Before You Continue**

1. **Problem/Solution** Why are starlings a problem in the United States?
2. **Make Inferences** Why do you think scientists believed that African bees would die in the forest?

Zebra Mussels

Many aliens arrive in the ballast tanks of cargo ships. Filled with seawater, these large tanks help ships stay balanced. The tanks are like **aquariums** in the middle of the ship. When a ship arrives in port, it empties its ballast tank. This action releases thousands of worms, clams, snails, and other sea creatures into an ecosystem where they do not belong.

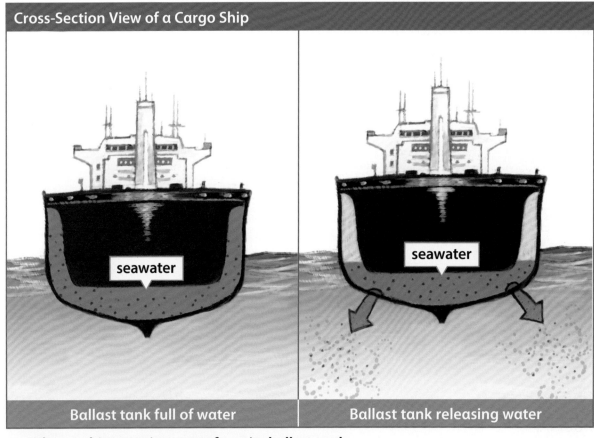

Cross-Section View of a Cargo Ship

seawater

seawater

Ballast tank full of water

Ballast tank releasing water

▲ When a ship empties water from its ballast tank, it may also release alien species into an ecosystem.

aquariums large fish tanks

◄ zebra mussels

Zebra **mussels** traveled from Europe to the United States on cargo ships in the late 1980's. Huge **populations** of these mussels live on **submerged** rocks, concrete, wood, and metal. They sink **buoys** and clog water pipes. They also eat the **plankton** on which local fish depend. There are so many zebra mussels that it is impossible to get rid of them. The United States now has rules to control the dumping of ballast water.

mussels shelled sea creatures, similar to clams
submerged underwater
buoys floating markers
plankton tiny sea animals

▶ Before You Continue
1. **Make Inferences** How do you think zebra mussels sink buoys?
2. **Problem/Solution** How did the United States solve the problem of ballast water?

Kudzu 〜〜

When people **introduced** kudzu to the United States, they **had good intentions**. Kudzu is a fast-growing green vine. The Japanese brought kudzu into the United States to decorate their **exhibit** at the 1876 Centennial Exposition in Philadelphia, Pennsylvania. Americans liked the beautiful vine with its sweet-smelling blossoms. Many people began planting it in their gardens.

In the 1930s, the U.S. government hired hundreds of workers to plant kudzu. People believed that the vine would help prevent soil from being washed away during rains.

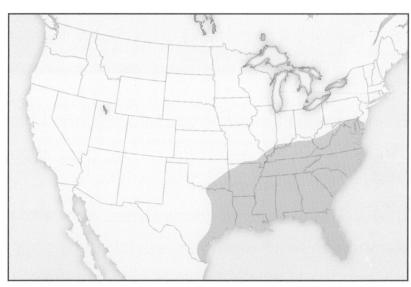

▲ **Kudzu has spread across the southeastern United States.**

had good intentions wanted to do something positive
exhibit display; show

No one realized that the warm, humid climate of the southeastern states was **more suitable** for kudzu than that of its **native** Japan. The vine can grow **up to** a foot a day. It covers millions of acres in the South. Kudzu severely damages forests. It covers trees and prevents them from getting sunlight.

▼ Kudzu vines compete with **native** plants.

kudzu

more suitable better
up to as much as

▶ Before You Continue
1. **Make Inferences** Why isn't kudzu a problem in Japan?
2. **Problem/Solution** How did the United States government make the kudzu problem worse?

Protecting Your Habitat

In today's world, travel is easy and quick. Living things can move from one ecosystem to another (or even from one continent to another) in a few hours. No part of our planet is **isolated** anymore. More aliens threaten **native** species than ever before.

The spread of alien **species** is a serious problem. People can take some simple steps to help solve it.

port

railway tracks

freeway

▲ Today, ships, cars, and trains can quickly and easily **introduce** alien **species** into an ecosystem.

isolated alone; separate from the rest

Here are some steps you can take:

- Learn to identify alien **species** in your area.

- Don't release exotic pets or aquarium plants and fish into the environment.

- Don't **disturb** natural areas.

- Do not send seeds, plants, or animals by mail if they could be harmful to the environment.

- When you travel, do not bring plants, fruits, soil, seeds, or animals from one country to another.

The place where you live is your **habitat**. You share it with many different kinds of animals and plants. You can help protect them and yourself from alien invaders. ❖

| Keep exotic pets in specific areas. | Learn to identify species in your area. | Help keep animals' natural habitats undisturbed. |

disturb interfere with

▶ **Before You Continue**

1. **Make Inferences** Why are **native species threatened** more than ever before?

2. **Problem/Solution** What is one way you can protect your **habitat** from alien invaders?

55

Think and Respond

Key Words	
balance	migration
competition	native
habitat	population
introduce	species
invade	threatened

Talk About It

1. What is the topic of this **science article**?
   Tell about two interesting details that support the topic.

   The topic is _____ . Two details are _____ and _____ .

2. How do alien plants and animals upset the **balance** in an ecosystem? **Define** words and phrases as you **explain**.

3. Sometimes people bring in alien **species** to fix one problem, but it causes another. Give an example of this from the text. Explain what happened.

Write About It

Which species from "Aliens from Earth" interests you the most? Write four questions that you could research to learn more about this species. Use **Key Words** to help you.

The species that interests me the most is _____ . My questions are:

1.

2.

3.

4.

Problem and Solution

Make a problem-and-solution chart for "Aliens from Earth." Give examples of the problem. Add boxes for more examples.

Problem-and-Solution Chart

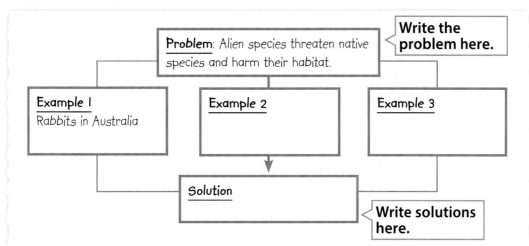

Work with a partner. Use your chart to summarize the problems and solutions presented in "Aliens from Earth." Be sure the author's meaning comes through in your summary. Use as many **Key Words** as you can.

> The problem is _____ .
> One example is _____ .
> One solution is _____ .

Fluency

Practice reading with phrasing. Rate your reading.

Talk Together

What makes some plants and animals harmful? Choose your favorite section of "Aliens from Earth." Make up a rap about that plant or animal. Use **Key Words** to tell how it became harmful.

Synonyms

Synonyms are words that have the same or nearly the same meaning, such as *grow* and *expand*. One word can have several synonyms. For example, *go*, *budge*, and *flow* are all synonyms for *move*.

Some **word analogies** use synonyms. You might not know the meaning of one of the words. But if you see that the words are synonyms, you can figure out an analogy.

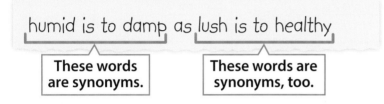

humid is to damp as lush is to healthy

| These words are synonyms. | These words are synonyms, too. |

The relationship between both pairs of words is the same.

Try It Together

Read each item. Choose the word that best completes the analogy.

1. **Threaten is to challenge as invade is to _____ .**

   A trap

   B species

   C escape

   D attack

2. **Population is to people as movement is to _____ .**

   A globe

   B population

   C migration

   D species

NATIONAL GEOGRAPHIC EXCLUSIVE

Island Observations

by Dr. Christy Finlayson

albatross

I am an ecologist, a scientist who studies how organisms **interact** with their environments. I'm also interested in the ways nonnative **species** affect an ecosystem.

I'm traveling to Midway Atoll, a group of three small islands in the Pacific Ocean. Midway Atoll is **very isolated**. Nonnative species have recently been **introduced** to the islands.

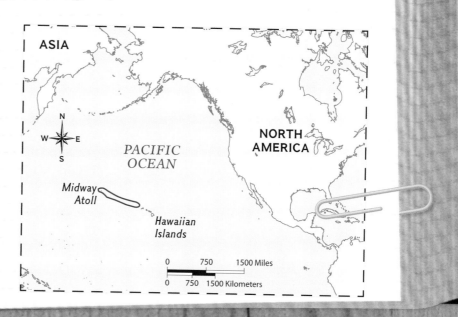

ASIA

NORTH AMERICA

PACIFIC OCEAN

Midway Atoll

Hawaiian Islands

| 0 | 750 | 1500 Miles |
| 0 | 750 | 1500 Kilometers |

interact act in a way that has an effect on another

very isolated separated from other places

▶ **Before You Continue**

1. **Make Inferences** Why do you think Dr. Finlayson is interested in Midway Atoll? What do you think she will study there?

2. **Use Text Features** Use the map to describe Midway Atoll's location.

September 6, 2007

I've arrived on Midway Atoll. Albatross chicks, a **native** seabird, are in nests everywhere! The adult birds feed them. They **regurgitate** partly eaten **squid** into their babies' mouths.

albatross

The Bonin petrel is another native seabird. It digs a **burrow** to lay its egg. If I don't pay attention, I could step on a burrow and crush it. So I walk carefully.

Once, more than 250,000 Bonin petrels lived here. Then humans accidentally brought rats to the islands. The rats preyed on the birds, which almost disappeared. Concerned scientists and citizens **eliminated** the rat **population**. Today, there are about 64,000 Bonin petrels on Midway Atoll.

▲ Ground-nesting birds, such as albatross and Bonin petrels, are everywhere on Midway Atoll.

◀ Bonin petrel and its burrow

▲ Adult albatross and chick

regurgitate spit up
◀ **squid** sea animal with eight short arms and two usually longer tentacles
burrow underground nest
eliminated destroyed

September 7, 2007

golden crownbeard

I've noticed that some areas have many birds. Other areas have few. I also notice a plant called golden crownbeard in the areas with few birds. This plant grows so thick that albatross have trouble walking. It also prevents Bonin petrels from digging their burrows.

When the golden crownbeard surrounds chicks in nests, adult birds may be unable to find them. The chicks can become trapped in the plant's stems and can **starve**.

People probably brought the golden crownbeard to Midway Atoll by accident. The plant's thick growth has decreased the nesting **habitat** for **native** ground-nesting birds.

▲ Albatross can't walk through the thick growth of the golden crownbeard.

▲ A thick growth of golden crownbeard

starve die of hunger

▶ **Before You Continue**

1. **Problem/Solution** Why were rats such a problem for Bonin petrels? What was the solution?

2. **Make Inferences** Is the golden crownbeard **native** to Midway Atoll? Explain.

September 8, 2007

I examined several golden crownbeard plants and noticed that there are many insects living in them. What are these organisms? Do they interact with the golden crownbeard and the ground-nesting seabirds?

I decided to **do a survey** of the insects in this plant **species**. For each plant I examine, I will **record** the name and number of each organism I find. Then I will write notes about the relationship between the organisms.

▲ **Insects on a golden crownbeard plant**

Survey of Insects on Golden Crownbeard

Stem Number	Organism	Number of Organisms	Notes
1	treehopper	6	treehoppers feeding on plant stem
1	crazy ant	13	ants feeding on **treehoppers' honeydew**
2	treehopper	14	treehoppers feeding on plant stem
2	crazy ant	29	ants feeding on treehoppers' honeydew
3	treehopper	2	treehoppers feeding on plant stem

do a survey take a sample
record write down
treehoppers' honeydew waste products from the insect's body

October 25, 2007

I observe three **species** of nonnative ants on golden crownbeard: crazy ants, tropical fire ants, and bigheaded ants. I know that some ants prey on ground-nesting seabirds. What is their connection with golden crownbeard, though?

golden crownbeard

The golden crownbeard provides food to treehoppers. The treehoppers provide food for the ants. From these observations, I **conclude** that the golden crownbeard is helping the ants that prey on **native** seabirds.

My next question: How can we prevent the ants from harming the seabird **populations** on Midway Atoll? ❖

▲ **At work on Midway Atoll**

---

conclude can tell; believe

▶ **Before You Continue**

1. **Use Text Features** Look at the chart on page 62. What relationship does the author observe between ants and treehoppers?

2. **Explain Ideas in the Text** What did the author learn from the survey?

Respond and Extend

Compare Genres

"Aliens from Earth" is a science text. "Island Observations" is a science journal. Think about their text features. How are they the same? How are they different? Work with a partner to complete the Venn diagram.

Venn Diagram

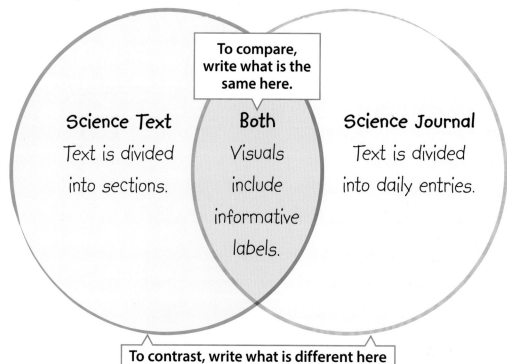

To compare, write what is the same here.

Science Text
Text is divided into sections.

Both
Visuals include informative labels.

Science Journal
Text is divided into daily entries.

To contrast, write what is different here

Talk Together

How can animals and plants become harmful? Think about the science text and science journal you just read. Use **Key Words** to talk about your ideas.

Possessive Nouns and Adjectives

A **possessive noun** is the name of an owner: *the **farmer's** crops.*
A **possessive adjective** can replace an owner's name: ***his** crops.*

Grammar Rules Possessive Nouns/Adjectives

	One Owner	**More Than One Owner**
Use an **apostrophe** with a possessive noun.	Add **'s**: the starling**'s** nest	Just add an apostrophe if the noun already ends in **-s**: the European**s'** cats Add **'s** if the noun does not end in **-s**: some people**'s** exotic pets
Choose the possessive adjective that matches the number of owners.	my your her, his, its	our your their

Read Possessive Nouns and Adjectives

Read these sentences from "Aliens from Earth." What possessive nouns and adjectives can you find? Show your partner.

> They also took cats to kill the rats that had arrived on settlers' ships. Their numbers grew quickly.

Write Possessive Nouns and Adjectives

Look at the picture on page 47. Write two sentences to describe what you see. Use possessive nouns and adjectives.

Write as a Citizen

Write a Persuasive Essay

How can you help protect your local ecosystem? Write an essay that persuades people to take action on an important issue. You will publish your essay in a Nature Newsletter.

Study a Model

In a persuasive essay, you give your opinion. You also try to influence what your readers think and do.

Read Kyle's essay about one thing people can do to protect local animals.

Pets as Pests

by Kyle Dushman

What happens when people get tired of pet fish or lizards? Sometimes they release them into a local pond. **They think they're being kind, but they aren't. They're actually hurting the ecosystem.**

The freed pets may carry diseases. The pets may also increase in number and eat the food that local animals need. The invaders may even attack or eat the wild animals!

If you have a pet you don't want anymore, don't release it. Instead, **find another owner for it**. You can even donate your pet to a school or daycare. The native animals in your community will thank you!

The essay begins with a description of a **problem**.

Next, Kyle gives **reasons** for his opinion.

Kyle states his **opinion**.

Finally, Kyle tells what **action** he wants people to take.

Prewrite

1. **Choose a Topic** What problem will you write about? Talk with a partner and choose a problem that you can help solve.

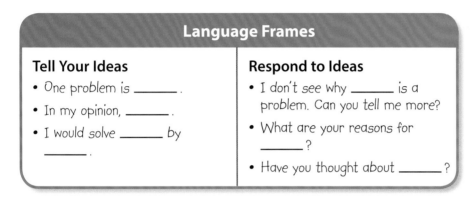

Language Frames	
Tell Your Ideas	**Respond to Ideas**
• One problem is _____ . • In my opinion, _____ . • I would solve _____ by _____ .	• I don't see why _____ is a problem. Can you tell me more? • What are your reasons for _____ ? • Have you thought about _____ ?

2. **Gather Information** Collect details that describe the problem. Write reasons for your opinion.

3. **Get Organized** Use a problem-and-solution chart to help you organize your ideas.

Problem-and-Solution Chart

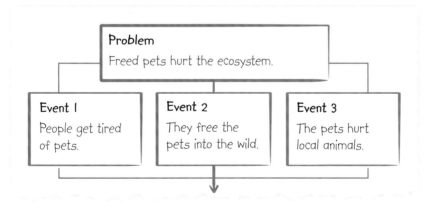

Problem
Freed pets hurt the ecosystem.

Event 1
People get tired of pets.

Event 2
They free the pets into the wild.

Event 3
The pets hurt local animals.

Draft

Use your chart to write your draft.

• Describe the problem and state your opinion.

• Support your opinion with reasons and details.

• End by telling your readers what you want them to do.

Revise

1. **Read, Retell, Respond** Read your draft aloud to a partner. Your partner listens and then retells your main points. Next, talk about ways to improve your writing.

Language Frames	
Retell	**Make Suggestions**
• The problem you're describing is _____ . You think _____ .	• I don't understand _____ . Can you say it in a different way?
• Your reasons for your opinion are _____ .	• Can you add more details about _____ ?
• You want people to _____ .	• I'm not sure what you want people to do. Maybe you could _____ .

2. **Make Changes** Think about your draft and your partner's suggestions. Then use revision marks to make your changes.

   • Did you state the problem and your opinion clearly?

   > They think they're being kind, but they aren't. They're actually hurting the ecosystem.
   > ∧ ~~This is a bad idea!~~

   • Make sure your readers will know what you want them to believe or do.

   > don't release it. Instead, find another owner for it.
   > If you have a pet you don't want anymore, ~~be careful what you~~ ∧ ~~do with it.~~

Spelling Tip

✔ Use *more* or *most* in front of longer adjectives instead of adding *-er* or *-est* to the end.

Edit and Proofread

Work with a partner to edit and proofread your persuasive essay. Check that you have used adjectives correctly to show comparison or ownership. Use revision marks to show your changes.

Present

On Your Own Make a final copy of your persuasive essay. Put the key points on note cards and present it to your class as a persuasive speech.

Presentation Tips	
If you are the speaker...	**If you are the listener...**
Remember that eye contact is important when you are persuading others.	Notice any persuasive techniques you think the speaker used well.
Be ready to support your opinion with additional reasons and examples.	Listen for specific words or phrases you think the speaker included to persuade you.

In a Group Collect all of the persuasive essays from your class. Publish them in a Nature Newsletter and share ideas with others in your school. You can also post your newsletter online in a blog.

Nature Newsletter

SPECIAL EDITION: Saving Our Local Ecosystem

Pets as Pests
by Kyle Dushman

What happens when people get tired of pet fish or lizards? Sometimes they release them into a local pond. They think they're being kind, but they aren't. They're actually hurting the ecosystem.

The freed pets may carry diseases. The pets may also increase in number and eat the food that local animals need.

When do harmless things become harmful?

Talk Together

In this unit, you found lots of answers to the **Big Question**. Now use your concept map to discuss the **Big Question** with the class.

Concept Map

Harmless Things that Become Harmful

mold

• invade ecosystems
•
•

Write a Paragraph

Look at your concept map. Choose one way that harmless things become harmful. Write a paragraph giving facts and information about it.

Share Your Ideas

Choose one of these ways to share your ideas about
the **Big Question**.

Write It!

Write a Play

Write a short play based on
"The Fungus That Ate My
School." Practice acting
out the
play with
a partner.

Talk About It!

Talk About Invasive Plants and Animals

Make up a story about an
invasive plant or animal.
Tell your story to a partner.
Then retell
your partner's
story to the
class.

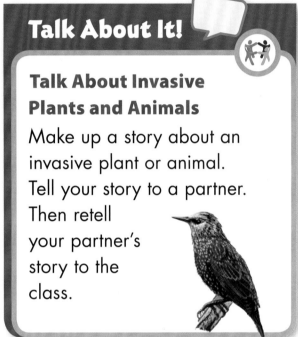

Do It!

Plant Seeds

Plant different kinds of seeds.
Keep a log to see which ones
grow fastest.

Write It!

Write about a Science Experiment

Think of a science
experiment to test an idea.
Write instructions for your
experiment.
Include
drawings.

Treasure Hunters

How do treasures shape our past and future?

INNER LAGOON, PALAU
A shipwreck now serving as an artificial reef that attracts marine life

Unit at a Glance
- **Language Focus**: Express Intentions, Restate an Idea
- **Reading Strategy**: Summarize, Identify the Main Idea and Details
- **Topic**: Exploration

Share What You Know

Do It!

1. **Make** a pirate ship from materials such as a box, construction paper, straws, clay, and colored markers.

2. **Display** your ship so everyone can see it.

3. **Tell** the class about your ship.

Express Intentions

Listen to Zack's chant. Then use **Language Frames** as you express the intention, or plan, to look for treasure.

Chant 🔊

My Treasure Hunt

There's treasure hiding here at home.

I'm going to discover it.

There's treasure hiding here at home.

I'm going to uncover it.

I plan to hunt in corners,
    under rugs, and inside drawers.

I plan to hunt on top of shelves
    and open unlocked doors.

I'll move the couch
    and look behind it.

If treasure's there,
    then I will find it!

Key Words

adventure

coastal

compass

navigation

port

treasure

◀)) Key Words

Look at the pictures. Use **Key Words** and other words to talk about the explorers who first came to the Americas by sea.

Exploring the New World

pirate

ship

treasure chest

coastal area

compass

Between 1500 and 1700, European explorers came to the Americas. They wanted land, gold, and other **treasures**. They found **adventure**. Some of the adventures involved pirates.

Explorers used tools such as maps and compasses for **navigation**. Some Europeans began to settle along the coasts of the Americas. They looked for good **ports** with deep water for their ships.

Talk Together

Why do you think explorers wanted treasure? With a group, try to use **Language Frames** from page 74 and **Key Words** as you express intentions.

Thinking Map

Characters

People grow and change. Story **characters** change, too. People's experiences and relationships can both cause the changes.

Look at the pictures of Zack and his little brother.

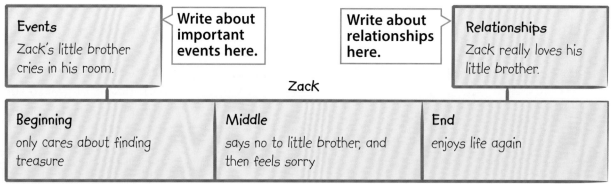

This is my real treasure!

Will you play?

I must find treasure!

Map and Talk

Make a character map to show how a person changes. Think about story events. Think about the character's relationships. Finally, think about how the character changes from beginning to middle to end.

Character Map

Events Zack's little brother cries in his room.	Write about important events here.	Write about relationships here.	Relationships Zack really loves his little brother.

Zack

Beginning only cares about finding treasure	Middle says no to little brother, and then feels sorry	End enjoys life again

Talk Together

Make a character map for one of your favorite characters from a story you know. Use the map to describe to a partner how the character changes.

◀)) More Key Words

Use these words to talk about "Treasure Island" and "Make a Treasure Map."

chart
noun

A **chart** shows information with numbers, pictures, words, and symbols. This **chart** is on a computer screen.

discovery
noun

When you find things, you make a **discovery**. Her **discovery** is a new germ.

exploration
noun

An **exploration** is a search. Astronauts learn about space from their **exploration**.

interpret
verb

To **interpret** something is to tell what you think it means. Can you **interpret** this road sign?

legend
noun

LEGEND	
⁓⁓⁓	Highway
⁓	Road
⁓	River
▦	Trees
▭	Swamp

A **legend** explains symbols on a map. This **legend** shows blue lines as rivers.

Talk Together

Work with a partner. Take turns telling a story using **Key Words**.

> We are going on an exploration.

> We hope to make a big discovery.

77

Learn to Summarize

Look at the picture. What does it show? What details do you notice? Now cover the picture. Think of a sentence or two that briefly tells, or **summarizes**, what the picture shows.

You **summarize** when you read, too.

How to Summarize

 1. Identify the topic. Ask, "What is this paragraph mostly about?"

 2. Take notes as you read. Determine which details are the most important.

 3. Use your notes to sum up the paragraph. Retell the ideas in a sentence or two.

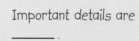

The topic is _____.

Important details are _____.

The paragraph _____.

Language Frames

❓ The topic is
_____ .

✏️ Important details
are _____ .

🧩 The paragraph
_____ .

Read Zack's essay, "Go for the Gold." Read the sample summary. Then use **Language Frames** to summarize each paragraph.

Essay

Go for the Gold

by Zack Jones

One winter, James Marshall made an amazing **discovery**. He found gold!

In 1847, Marshall began building a sawmill for a man named Sutter. The next January, Marshall saw some bright flakes in the water coming from the mill. Many people would have ignored the flakes. Not Marshall. He knew how to **interpret** the signs. He thought the flakes were gold. No one believed him at first, but he was right!

Sutter's sawmill was in California. Word spread fast. About 300,000 people came to California to join the **exploration** for gold. People called it the Gold Rush. They followed **charts** and maps to find **treasure**. Of course, not everyone got rich. Marshall never made any money from his discovery.

You can visit the spot where the Gold Rush started. Today, the area is a state park. Use the map **legend** to find the way. Visitors can have their own **adventures**. Maybe you will strike it rich!

Sample Summary

"The topic is James Marshall's discovery.

Important details are Marshall building a sawmill and finding bright flakes in the water.

The paragraph is about how James Marshall discovered gold."

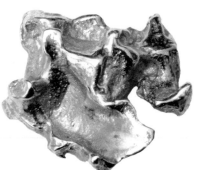

piece of gold ▶

◀ = A good place to summarize

Read a Play

Genre

A **play** is a story that actors can perform on a stage. The actors pretend to be characters in the story.

Elements of Drama

The parts of a play are called **scenes**. Each scene describes the setting. **Stage directions** can tell the characters how to talk, act, or move. The words the characters say are called the **dialogue**.

scene ⟩ **SCENE ONE**

[**SETTING** *The play begins in a small coastal town in England, around 1740. The Admiral Benbow* **Inn***, a common gathering place among sailors.* BILLY BONES, *looking ill, lies on a couch.* MRS. HAWKINS **tends to** *him.* JIM *and* DR. LIVESEY *enter.*]

JIM [*talks to* DR. LIVESEY, *but points to* BILLY]: He's been here eight months. Billy never gave us any trouble.

stage directions

MRS. HAWKINS: Dr. Livesey, thank goodness you've come!

dialogue

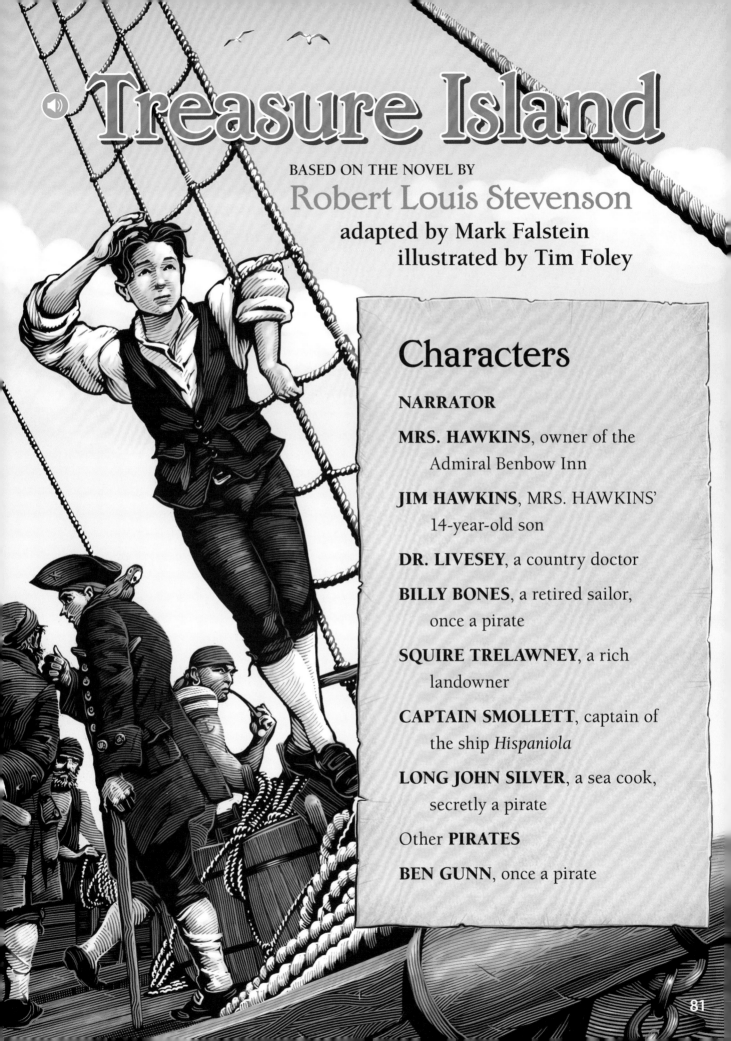

Treasure Island

BASED ON THE NOVEL BY

Robert Louis Stevenson

adapted by Mark Falstein
illustrated by Tim Foley

Characters

NARRATOR

MRS. HAWKINS, owner of the Admiral Benbow Inn

JIM HAWKINS, MRS. HAWKINS' 14-year-old son

DR. LIVESEY, a country doctor

BILLY BONES, a retired sailor, once a pirate

SQUIRE TRELAWNEY, a rich landowner

CAPTAIN SMOLLETT, captain of the ship *Hispaniola*

LONG JOHN SILVER, a sea cook, secretly a pirate

Other **PIRATES**

BEN GUNN, once a pirate

▶ Set a Purpose
Find out about a **discovery** that
leads to **adventure**.

SCENE ONE

[**SETTING** *The play begins in a small* **coastal** *town
in England, around 1740. The Admiral Benbow* **Inn***, a
common gathering place among sailors. BILLY BONES,
looking ill, lies on a couch. MRS. HAWKINS* **tends to**
him. JIM and DR. LIVESEY enter.]

JIM [*talks to* DR. LIVESEY, *but points to* BILLY]:
He's been here eight months. Billy never gave us
any trouble.

MRS. HAWKINS: Dr. Livesey, thank goodness
you've come!

LIVESEY: Let's have a look at him. Young Jim said that
a blind man came looking for Billy?

MRS. HAWKINS: Yes, he gave him this paper. Billy
had a fit when he saw it. Then he **collapsed**.

LIVESEY [*looks at the paper and gasps*]: The black spot!
That's a pirate sign!

JIM: Pirates?

BILLY [*weak*]: Jim, is that you?

JIM: Yes, Billy, and Dr. Livesey's here.

Inn Hotel
tends to takes care of
had a fit was very upset
collapsed fell down ill

BILLY: Jim, Flint's **crew is** coming for me! The packet is in my **sea chest**. Don't let them get it!

[BILLY **shudders** and lies still. DR. LIVESEY examines him.]

LIVESEY: He's dead—frightened to death, most likely. His crimes have caught up with him if he sailed with Captain Flint. They were the most **bloodthirsty** pirates on the seas!

MRS. HAWKINS [*frightened*]: And they're coming here!

crew is sailors are
sea chest sailor's
 storage box ▶
shudders shakes
bloodthirsty
 terrible; cruel

[*Lights fade, showing that time is passing.*]

NARRATOR: That night, pirates *did* come to the inn. They found Billy's sea chest, but Jim had hidden the packet. The next day, Dr. Livesey returned with Squire Trelawney.

[*Lights on.* JIM, DR. LIVESEY, *and* SQUIRE TRELAWNEY *sit at a table.* JIM *unwraps a packet.*]

TRELAWNEY: You've done a man's job, Jim! Let's see what Captain Flint's men were looking for.

[JIM *unfolds a map. They stare at it.*]

LIVESEY: It's a map of an island.

JIM [*pointing*]: Look! It shows a **treasure** here!

TRELAWNEY: This must be Flint's map!

LIVESEY: You're a brave **lad**, Jim! Those pirates would have done anything to get this!

TRELAWNEY: Captain Flint's treasure! There's a fortune in gold and jewels! And we have the map!

LIVESEY: What should we do with it?

TRELAWNEY: Do? Why, I'll hire a ship! Then we're **bound for** Treasure Island! Jim, you and your mother will be rich!

JIM: Us? Rich?

TRELAWNEY: Why, certainly! You're sailing with us, aren't you?

---

treasure wealth, rich materials, or valuable things
lad boy
bound for going to

▶ **Before You Continue**

1. **Summarize** What important **discovery** do the characters make in Scene One?
2. **Character** How would you describe the relationship between Jim and Livesey? Explain.

▶ **Predict**
What will happen on the journey
to Treasure Island?

SCENE TWO

[**SETTING** *Aboard the ship* Hispaniola. JIM, DR. LIVESEY, SQUIRE TRELAWNEY, *and* CAPTAIN SMOLLETT *are in the captain's cabin. A large barrel sits on the deck.*]

SMOLLETT: We'll reach the island tomorrow.

JIM: And then we'll be rich!

LIVESEY: We've been lucky. The sea has been calm, and the crew has been **lively**.

TRELAWNEY: We can thank Long John Silver for finding the crew. It's a good thing I found *him*! He's only a cook, but those tough sailors respect him.

JIM: He tells interesting stories, too.

SMOLLETT [*worried*]: Yes, he **favors** you.

LIVESEY: Jim, would you **fetch** me an apple?

JIM: Aye-aye, Doctor.

[JIM *exits the cabin and walks to the barrel. He reaches into the barrel but can't reach the apples. He climbs in, just as* LONG JOHN SILVER *and other* PIRATES *enter.* SILVER *has a wooden leg. A parrot perches on his shoulder.*]

lively excited and full of energy
favors likes
fetch get
Aye-aye Yes

SILVER [*talks quietly to* PIRATES]: No, it was Flint. He was captain. I was **second-in-command**. If I knew where the **treasure** was buried, I'd be dead, like old Ben Gunn!

FIRST PIRATE: I still say we should kill them and take the map!

SILVER: And who will bring the ship home? None of us can **set a course**. No, we should let them dig up the treasure. When we're halfway home, then we'll **strike**!

SECOND PIRATE: Aye! And then we'll live like kings!

second-in-command next in charge
set a course find the way back
strike attack

[PIRATES *exit, laughing.* JIM *climbs out of the barrel and runs to the cabin.*]

JIM [*excited*]: They're pirates!

SMOLLETT: Who?

JIM: The crew! I heard them talking. Silver is their leader! They plan to **seize** the ship and steal the **treasure**!

TRELAWNEY [**stunned**]: This is my fault. I never should have told anyone we were **after** treasure.

LIVESEY: That doesn't matter now. We'll have to fight them.

seize take control of
stunned shocked
after looking for

SMOLLETT [*looks at the* **treasure** *map*]: Gentlemen, I have a plan. The map shows a **fort** on the island. I'll give the crew some free time on shore. They can take a rowboat. Then *we'll* go **ashore** and **occupy** the fort.

[*Lights fade.*]

NARRATOR: Jim had his own plan. He hid in the rowboat under a piece of sail cloth. The pirates rowed to the island, eager for treasure. As soon as they **touched** land, Jim jumped out of the rowboat.

fort a strong building to keep out intruders
ashore to the island
occupy stay in
touched arrived on

▶ **Before You Continue**

1. **Character** What does Jim find out about the crew on the journey to Treasure Island? How does this change him?

2. **Elements of Drama** Where does Scene Two take place? Explain how you know.

▶ **Predict**
If there *is* **treasure**, who will get it, and how?

SCENE THREE

[**SETTING** *The island. Sand and palm trees.*]

[JIM *runs across the stage.*]

SILVER [*from offstage*]: Jim, Jim! Come back!

JIM: No chance of that, you pirate!

[*The* PIRATES *rush onstage, followed by* SILVER.]

FIRST PIRATE: *I'll* fetch him back!

SILVER: Don't hurt him!

JIM [*to himself*]: I thought he was my friend! I'll never trust him again!

[*The* PIRATES *chase* JIM. JIM *runs offstage, followed by the* PIRATES.]

JIM [*enters from offstage, alone and out of breath*]: I think I've lost them. [*hopeless*] I was foolish. Why didn't I stay with my friends? [*points **upstage***] There's a cave! I'll hide there!

[JIM *goes into the cave.* BEN GUNN *enters the cave from offstage.*]

JIM and BEN [*surprised*]: Oh!

BEN: Are you real, boy? Who are you?

JIM: I'm Jim Hawkins. Who are *you*?

BEN: I'm Ben Gunn. For three years I've been alone here!

JIM: Were you shipwrecked?

BEN: No, I was **marooned**, left here to die. I stayed alive by trapping wild goats. What I wouldn't give for a bit of toasted cheese! [*grabs* JIM's *arm*] Tell me **true**, boy! Is that Flint's ship out there?

upstage toward the back of the stage
marooned left on shore alone
true the truth

JIM: No, Flint's dead. Some of his crew are **on board**, though. They're after Flint's **treasure**.

BEN: Hee-hee, they won't find it! [*suddenly scared*] I hope they don't find *me!*

JIM: Ben, I have friends here. They are at the fort now. Can we get to the fort without being seen?

BEN: Flint's fort? Hee-hee, I know a secret path. Come, Jim!

[*Lights fade.*]

NARRATOR: Ben led Jim to the fort. That night, the pirates attacked the fort. Jim **slipped away**. But when he returned, the pirates were in control of the fort. Ben Gunn and his friends were gone! The pirates captured Jim.

[*Lights on. Another part of the island.* SILVER *holds the map with one hand. With the other hand, he holds* JIM *by the elbow. Nearby,* PIRATES *are digging.*]

SILVER: Ah, Jim, your friends became as gentle as lambs when they thought I had you. The doctor traded the map for your safety. Well, I didn't have you then, but I do now! [*to the* PIRATES] Dig, you lazy dogs!

SECOND PIRATE: Here, we've struck something!

FIRST PIRATE: It's a treasure chest!

SILVER: Haul it up!

on board on the ship
slipped away escaped
Haul Pull

[PIRATES *pull up the* **treasure** *chest.* SILVER **knocks back** *the lid. They stare inside.*]

FIRST PIRATE: Two gold coins? That's Flint's treasure? *Two coins?*

SILVER: There must be a mistake!

SECOND PIRATE: We trusted you! *That* was *our* mistake!

knocks back opens

95

[JIM **breaks free** and runs offstage. Lights fade. Sound of pirates fighting. When the lights come back on, SQUIRE TRELAWNEY, DR. LIVESEY, CAPTAIN SMOLLETT–and BEN GUNN–are waiting by a rowboat. They are carrying heavy sacks. JIM enters.]

TRELAWNEY: Jim! Jim, you're safe!

JIM: Hurry! They'll be after me!

[They all climb into the boat.]

LIVESEY: Your friend Ben tells us he had the treasure . I knew the map was useless.

BEN: [holds up a sack] I hid it in my cave! But how could I spend it here?

JIM: You can buy all the toasted cheese you want now!

TRELAWNEY: And those pirates will be **stuck** here!

SMOLLETT: To the ship, now! Row!

JIM: Aye-aye, Captain! ❖

breaks free escapes
stuck trapped

▶ **Before You Continue**
1. **Summarize** Who gets the treasure in the end? How?
2. **Character** How does Ben help Jim? What does this tell you about Ben's character?

Robert Louis Stevenson

The play "Treasure Island" is based on a book by Robert Louis Stevenson. Stevenson was born in Scotland in 1850. When he was young, Stevenson was often sick, and Scotland's cold, foggy climate was bad for his health. When he grew up, he traveled to warm islands like the ones he wrote about in his adventure books. Later in his life, Stevenson moved to the island of Upolu, in Samoa. There he was called *Tusitala*, or *Teller of Tales*.

The story "Treasure Island" began as a homemade map of a made-up island. The map grew into a story idea, and the story idea grew into a book about buried treasure, pirates, and adventure. The book was a big success.

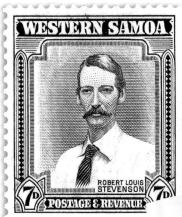

◀ A portrait of Robert Louis Stevenson appears on a Western Samoan postal stamp.

Writing Tip

Stevenson created many colorful characters for his story. Look at some of the characters in the play. Then write a short description of a new character that could be part of the story.

Think and Respond

Key Words

adventure	interpret
chart	legend
coastal	navigation
compass	port
discovery	treasure
exploration	

Talk About It

1. If you were an actor in this **play**, how would you know how to move or speak on the stage? Use two examples as you explain.

   Actors use _____ to tell them how to speak and move. For example, _____ .

2. Imagine that you are Ben Gunn and that you have just met Jim. **Express intentions** about what you will do.

   Here's my plan, Jim. I am going to _____ . I will _____ .

3. How do you think Long John Silver feels after he opens the **treasure** chest? Why?

   Long John Silver feels _____ because _____ . I think this because _____ .

Write About It ✏️

Think about Jim's **adventure**. Compare it to the adventures of another character from a story you have read. Write a paragraph to compare the characters' adventures. Use **Key Words** and examples to explain your points.

> The adventure that Jim experienced was _____ .

Characters

Make a character map for Jim, the main character in "Treasure Island." Show how he changes.

Character Map

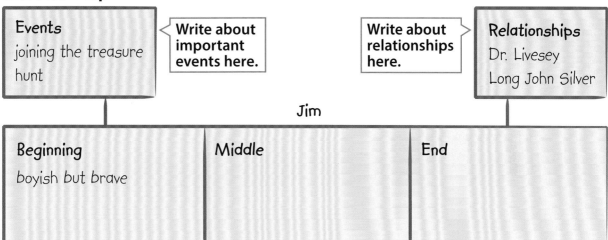

Now use your **chart** as you retell the story to a partner. Focus on Jim and how he changes. Use as many **Key Words** as you can. If possible, record your retelling.

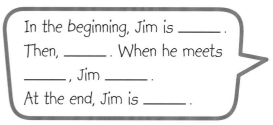

In the beginning, Jim is _____ . Then, _____ . When he meets _____ , Jim _____ . At the end, Jim is _____ .

Fluency

Practice reading with expression. Rate your reading.

Talk Together

Why did Jim and his friends seek **treasure**? Role-play an interview with Jim and his friends. Talk about why they left England aboard the ship. Try to use **Key Words**.

Prefixes

A **prefix** is a word part at the beginning of a word. Many prefixes come from other languages such as Latin or Greek. A prefix changes the meaning of the word.

The prefix **mis-** means "bad" or "wrongly."

| mis- | + | interpret | = | misinterpret |

When you **misinterpret** something, you understand wrongly.

Prefix	Origin	Meaning	Example
dis-	Latin	opposite	disagree
micro-	Greek	small	microscope
re-	Latin	again	rebuild
under-	Old English	below	underwater

Try It Together

Read the sentences. Use the chart above to answer the questions.

The explorers told of their <u>misadventures</u>. Their boat had <u>disappeared</u> in a storm. It drifted toward the coast.

1. What does <u>misadventure</u> mean?
   A an adventure that was fun
   B an adventure that went wrong
   C an adventure in the cold
   D an adventure at sea

2. What does <u>disappear</u> mean?
   A to show up again
   B to show up underwater
   C to move out of view
   D to move out of view again

Making Connections Make your own **treasure** map! Read these instructions.

Genre **Instructions** tell how to do something or make something. They usually include steps to follow in a certain order.

Make a Treasure Map

adapted from the
New England Pirate Museum Website

Many **adventure** stories tell about pirates who buried chests of **treasure** on uninhabited islands—faraway places where no one lived. The pirates created maps so they could locate the buried treasure. The maps showed details about the island, such as hills, lakes, and trees. A large X marked the spot where the treasure was buried. A line may have shown a path to the treasure.

▶ **Before You Continue**

1. **Summarize** What is a treasure map? What is the most important thing it shows?
2. **Use Text Features** Look at the map. Where is the treasure buried?

101

Materials

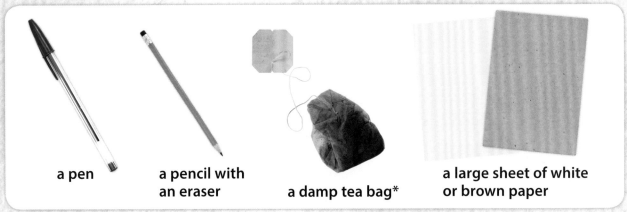

a pen
a pencil with
an eraser
a damp tea bag*
a large sheet of white
or brown paper

* You can use brown paper in place of the white paper and tea bag. **Crumple** the brown paper to make it look old and worn.

Steps

1. Use a pencil to **sketch** the shape of your island on the paper.

2. On your island, draw symbols for the following: hills, lakes, trees, water, and your **treasure**. Then draw a map **legend** that tells what each symbol represents.

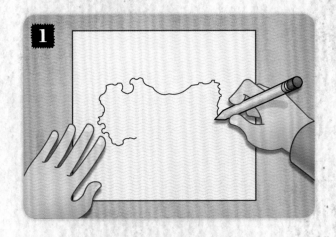

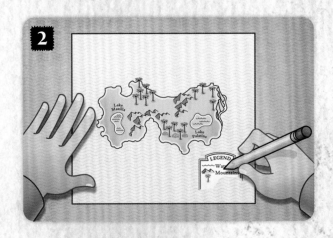

◀ **Crumple** Crush
sketch lightly draw

3. Draw a **compass rose** in one corner of the map.

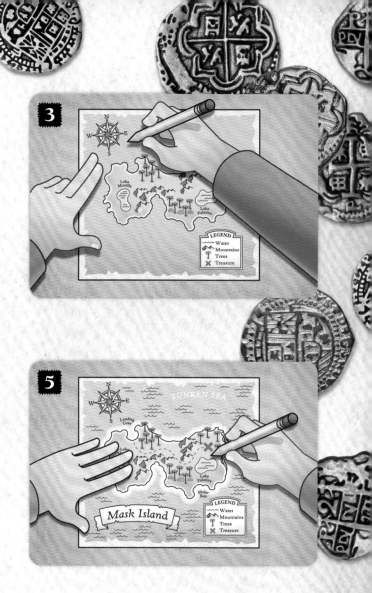

4. Make up a name for your island, the ocean that surrounds it, and any coves or bays where ships can land. Write labels for all of these places.

5. Mark the location of the buried **treasure** with an X.

6. Show a path from the ship to the treasure. Use a dotted line.

7. When your map is finished, trace over the pencil lines with a pen.

8. Rub a damp tea bag over your map to make it look old. Let the map dry. Then fold the map carefully and tear the edges to make it look **worn**. ❖

compass rose symbol that shows north, east, south, west ▶

worn used; old

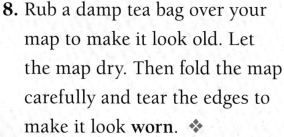

▶ **Before You Continue**

1. **Summarize** How do you make a **treasure** map?

2. **Steps in a Process** In what order do you use the materials when making the map?

Key Words

adventure	interpret
chart	legend
compass	navigation
coastal	port
discovery	treasure
exploration	

Compare Texts

Some maps show roads and cities. Others show natural features like mountains and oceans. How are the **treasure** maps in the play and in the instructions similar? How are they different? Work with a partner to complete the Venn diagram.

Venn Diagram

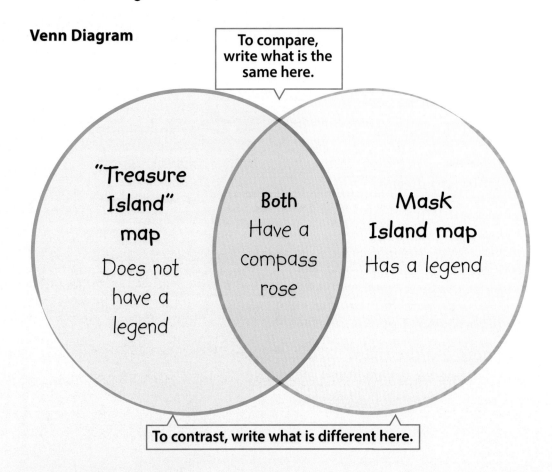

To compare, write what is the same here.

"Treasure Island" map

Does not have a legend

Both

Have a compass rose

Mask Island map

Has a legend

To contrast, write what is different here.

Talk Together

What makes people want to search for treasure? Think about the play you read and the treasure map you learned how to make. Use **Key Words** to talk about your ideas.

Pronoun Agreement

Use the right **subject pronoun**, **object pronoun**, or **reflexive pronoun**.

Grammar Rules Pronoun Agreement

	One	More Than One
• Use for yourself.	I, me, myself	
• Use for yourself and one or more persons.		we, us, ourselves
• Use when you speak to one or more persons.	you, you, yourself	you, you, yourselves
• Use for one other person or thing.	he, she, it him, her, it himself, herself, itself	
• Use for more than one other person or thing.		they, them, themselves

Read Pronouns

Read this passage. Find the pronouns.

> SILVER: Don't hurt him!
> JIM [to himself]: I thought he was my friend!

Write Pronouns

What do you own that is a treasure? Write a conversation you might have. Tell about your treasure. Use pronouns.

Restate an Idea

Listen to Lucia's song. Then use **Language Frames** as you restate an idea about looking for treasure.

Language Frames

- From _____ , I know _____ .
- In other words, _____ .

Song

Bongo's Treasure Hunt

My dog Bongo, my dog Bongo,
Dropped his bone in a hole.
But he is a neat pup,
So he filled the hole up.
Then he ran off to play.

When my dog returned to find it,
He could not find the bone.
He sniffed all around it.
Finally he found it,
In the ground, in the ground.

Tune: "Frère Jacques"

From watching Bongo, I know that he buried a bone, lost it, and then found it. In other words, he found buried treasure!

Key Words

archaeologist

artifact

currency

galleon

merchant

🔊 Key Words

Look at the picture. Use **Key Words** and other words to talk about archaeology. This field of study looks at how people lived in the past.

galleon

merchants

archaeologist

An **archaeologist** looks at **artifacts** from a 300-year-old Spanish **galleon**. Long ago, **merchants** sent their goods across the sea on these ships.

Coins tell about **currency** used in the past.

Talk Together

Why do archaeologists look for treasure? Try to use Language Frames from page 106 and **Key Words** to restate an idea to a partner.

Sequence

When things happen in a certain order, they are in **sequence**. When you talk about sequence, use

- time-order words: *first, next, then, finally*
- days, months, seasons
- dates

Look at the pictures of a treasure hunt.

Map and Talk

You can make a timeline to show the order of events. Here's how you make one. Write the first event beside the first line. At the next line, describe what happens next, and so on.

Timeline

Bongo looks at a treasure map that Lucia drew.

He takes the map with him to find the treasure.

He digs a hole.

He finds the treasure. It's a bone!

Talk Together

Did you ever lose an object that was important to you? Make a timeline that shows how you tried to find the lost object. Describe the events in order. Tell your partner about your timeline.

🔊 More Key Words

Use these words to talk about "Diving for Treasure" and "La Belle Shipwreck."

colony
noun

A **colony** is a region that another country controls. These U.S. states were once **colonies** of Great Britain.

examine
verb

To **examine** something is to look at it closely. With a magnifying glass, you can **examine** a butterfly.

preserve
verb

To **preserve** something is to keep it safe from harm. Use photo albums to **preserve** old pictures.

route
noun

A **route** is a path to go someplace. Do you take the shortest **route** to school?

trade
verb

To **trade** is to exchange one thing for another. The friends **trade** toys.

Talk Together

Work with a partner. Make a Word Web for each **Key Word**.

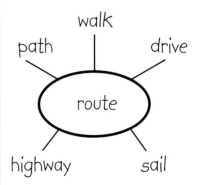

walk
path
drive
route
highway
sail

Identify the Main Idea and Details

Look at the picture. What is it mostly about? Think of a sentence that tells the **main idea**. What **details** support the main idea?

You look for **main ideas** and **details** when you read, too.

How to Identify the Main Idea and Details

👁	**1.** Identify the topic. Look at the title, pictures, captions, and repeated words for clues.
☁	**2.** Read the text. What does it mainly say about the topic?
🧩	**3.** Look at the details. How do they support the main idea?

The topic is _____ .

The main idea is _____ .

Important details are _____ .

Read the biography that Lucia wrote. Read the sample, too. Then use **Language Frames** as you identify the main idea and details for the other paragraphs in the biography.

Biography

A 16th-Century Treasure Hunter

by Lucia Vargas

Francisco Vázquez de Coronado was born in Spain in 1510. When he was 25, he made an important choice. He went to Spain's **colony** in Mexico. There he heard about seven cities of gold. Coronado wanted to find gold to bring back to Spain.

In 1540, he led a team to find this treasure. The team included 300 Spanish soldiers and more than 1,000 Native Americans. They carried goods to **trade**. Their **route** passed through land that is now Texas, Arizona, New Mexico, Kansas, and Oklahoma.

Coronado never found gold. However, he influenced history. He was a powerful person and part of a government council in Mexico City. A writer kept an account of Coronado's travels in search of gold. This account was **preserved** and later published. Some readers **examined** it for clues about the treasure. So, although he did not get rich, Coronado probably inspired other people to hunt for treasure.

Sample

"The topic is Coronado's search for gold.

The main idea is that Coronado explored new lands.

Important details are that he went to Mexico and heard about seven cities of gold.

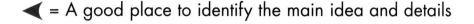
◄ = A good place to identify the main idea and details

111

Read a History Article

Genre

A **history article** is nonfiction. It gives facts about people and events from the past.

Text Feature

Illustrations in a history article can help you visualize people and events from long ago, before photography was invented.

▲ Alan Villiers with Captain Ali bin Nasr al-Nejdi

Diving
for
Treasure

The Story of Pearl Divers in the Middle East

adapted by **Eloise Vivanco** *from information recorded by* **Alan Villiers**

▶ **Set a Purpose**
Find out who Alan Villiers was
and what he did.

Who was Alan Villiers?

The **call of** the sea can be very strong. So can the call of the pen. Fortunately, Alan Villiers heard both calls. He was a **mariner**, a writer, and a photographer, but most of all, he was an adventurer.

In his life, Villiers published many books and articles, all of them based on his adventures at sea. He **documented** every voyage with both words and photos. The **volume** of work he left to the world is truly **astounding**.

Alan Villiers ▶

call of the power to attract someone
mariner sailor
documented wrote about
volume amount
astounding amazing

Born in Australia in 1903, Villiers was interested in sailing from a very young age. He would watch ships sail in and out of the Port of Melbourne and dream of sailing them one day.

When he was only fifteen, young Alan became an apprentice on the **barque** *Rothesay Bay*. He loved it very much, and in 1923, he made a voyage to the Antarctic. By the age of 21, he was a professional sailor, **setting out** in search of adventure.

Villiers lived in a time of **industrialization**. Steamships were replacing the sailing boats he loved in many countries. But not in the Arab world where sailing was still the norm.

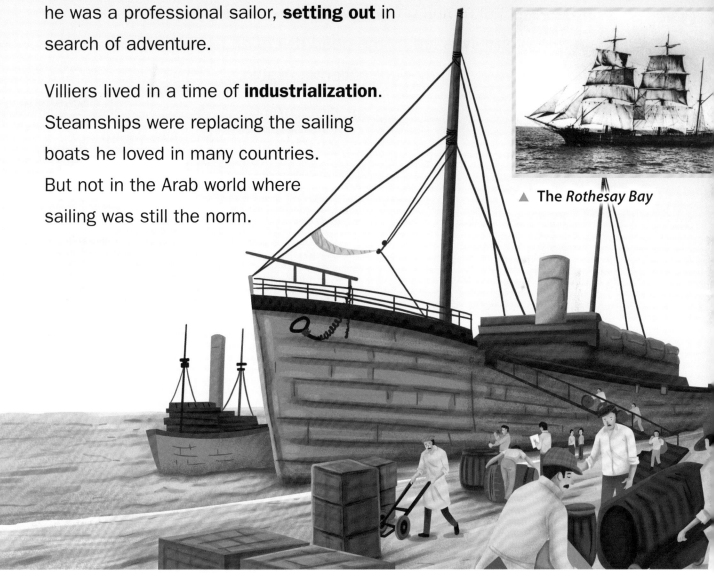

▲ The *Rothesay Bay*

barque a type of sailing ship
setting out beginning a journey
industrialization modernization; development

▶ **Before You Continue**
1. **Details** What does the writer find interesting about Alan Villiers?
2. **Sequence** List events in Alan Villier's life as they occurred.

As a writer and photographer, Villier's experiences gave him much to **chronicle**. He wanted to **examine** and record the way of life aboard traditional sailing ships. He spent a year at sea with sailors from Kuwait, which led him to write a book called *"Sons of Sindbad."*

The book is filled with pictures and stories about the highs and lows of life at sea on a Kuwaiti **dhow**. It details the incredibly hard lives led by the pearl divers on board, or the ***ghai ghawwas***, as they were called in Arabic.

Seaman and photographer Alan Villiers ▶

▲ **A traditional Arab dhow, Egypt, 1930**

chronicle record in writing and photographs

dhow a traditional Arabian sailing ship

ghai ghawwas pearl divers

Alan Villiers boarded the *Bayan* in the port of Kuwait as a crewman in 1938. The dhow was taking a **route** from the Arabian Gulf to East Africa, carrying a cargo of dates. The captain, Ali bin Nasr al-Nejdi, was a bit **suspicious** of Villiers and why he wanted to take part in this journey, but he decided to allow him aboard. They soon developed a good relationship, and Villiers **documented** the crew's **spirit** and their ability to work in **extremely** difficult conditions.

Alan Villiers and Captain Ali bin Nasr al-Nejdi ▼

▼ **The** *Bayan*

suspicious distrustful
documented recorded
spirit positive attitude and energy
extremely very

▶ **Before You Continue**

1. **Make Inferences** Why do you think the captain was suspicious? Why do you think he decided to let Villiers aboard?

2. **Use Text Features** What does the illustration tell you about Villiers and the captain?

▶ **Set a Purpose**
Find out what conditions were like aboard the dhow.

Villiers had already owned and **captained** a ship of his own. His **status** meant that he was not treated as an ordinary crew member. He shared the **poop deck** with high-ranking members of the crew and important passengers such as **merchants**. However, the rest of the crew and passengers, including women and children, lived in very **cramped conditions** for the entire journey. The voyages lasted many weeks—the fishing season was between May and September—so the passengers and crew **endured** many hardships.

captained been in charge of
status importance
poop deck the highest deck on a ship
cramped conditions uncomfortably small living space
endured suffered

Pearl Diving

Some of the crew members were pearl divers. Villiers was fascinated by these men, who risked their lives to find treasure deep in the sea. He wrote detailed descriptions of their dangerous dives and took many photos of the divers.

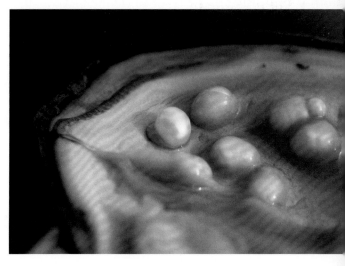

▲ **Pearls in an oyster shell**

In his book, Villiers writes about how pearls are formed inside an oyster's shell when some kind of **irritant,** such as a **parasite,** gets inside. The oyster protects itself by coating the irritant in a substance called *nacre*. The layers of nacre form to make a beautiful pearl, which is sometimes known as *the jewel of the sea*.

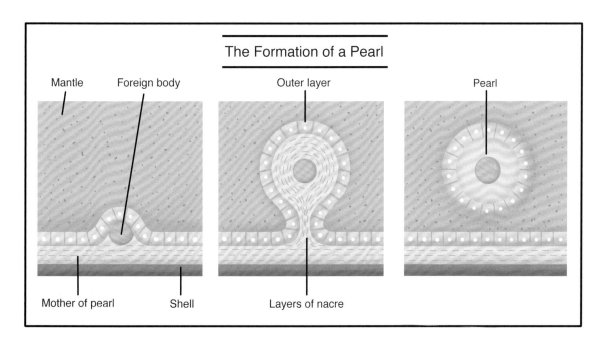

The Formation of a Pearl

Mantle   Foreign body   Outer layer   Pearl

Mother of pearl   Shell   Layers of nacre

irritant something that makes the oyster uncomfortable

parasite an organism that feeds on its host

▶ **Before You Continue**

1. **Recording Evidence** How did Villiers record his experience? What tools did he use?

2. **Sequence** What are the stages of a pearl forming? In what order do they happen?

Pearl divers collected the oysters from the bottom of the sea to **extract** the pearls. This was a difficult and dangerous job. The divers used oil to coat their skin and protect themselves from stings or scrapes. The oil also kept them warm. They put cotton wool in their ears and wore nose clips to keep the water from getting in. They also wore leather **sheathes** on their fingers and toes to protect them from the sharp rocks.

extract remove
sheathes protective coverings

The divers held a heavy rock with a rope tied around it to sink down to find the **oyster beds**. They often went as deep as 18 meters, which is **roughly** the height of a six-story building! They hung a basket around their necks to collect the oysters and bring them back to the boat.

Some divers could go as deep as 26 meters, which was very dangerous. They had no equipment to help them breathe. A diver just held his breath, scraped the oysters off the rocks with a knife, and put them in his basket.

oyster beds places where oysters live
roughly approximately

▶ **Before You Continue**
1. **Main Idea** What are the main reasons that pearl diving was dangerous?
2. **Make Connections** What challenges do you think pearl divers faced? How might they have overcome these challenges?

The divers had an assistant on the boat called the *saib*. The saib was in training to be a pearl diver. He would pull up the ropes tied to the stones to help the divers rise to the surface.

The divers went down many times a day—sometimes as often as 30! With up to 40 divers on some boats, they could get as many as 8,000 oysters a day! The divers had to dive so much because only around one percent of the oysters they **retrieved** contained a pearl. Each oyster had to be opened on the deck to discover which ones contained the valuable treasure.

retrieved brought back

The captain was responsible for keeping all the pearls to sell them. He kept them in a special red cloth. The pearls sold for a lot of money, but the divers received a very small **portion** of the **profits**. The divers were very poor, and if they didn't find enough pearls, they would actually be **in debt** to the captain at the end of the fishing season.

To board the dhow, the divers had to pay the captain a fee, which they repaid by finding pearls. The captains were in debt, too— to pearl **merchants** who had loaned them money to pay for the voyages. So finding as many pearls as possible was very important.

portion part
profits earnings
in debt owe money

▶ **Before You Continue**

1. **Sequence** When did pearl divers receive money? When did they have to pay?
2. **Use Text Features** Look at the illustrations on pages 122–123. What do they help you understand?

On the other hand, if a pearl diver found a lot of pearls, then he may have earned enough money to buy land for his family and escape **poverty**. This dangerous job gave divers the chance to give their families a better life, but it was also very **risky**. Many pearl divers lost their lives. To make the journey more **bearable,** there was a special singer on board each dhow, called a *nahham*. The nahham sang songs and prayers to comfort and **motivate** the divers. His music also provided a rhythm for the rowers to follow.

The nahham sings a song for the divers ▼

On the other hand However
poverty being very poor
risky dangerous
bearable tolerable
motivate inspire

Villiers was very **fortunate** to have journeyed on the last traditional ships in the Arabian Gulf and to have recorded what life aboard was like. His writing and photos meant that thousands of readers around the world can imagine what life was like at sea in the 1930s.

World War II started in Europe in 1939 and Villiers's voyage in the Gulf was over. He served as a commander in the British navy because his home country, Australia, used to be a **colony** of Great Britain. This was an entirely different type of adventure, but he never stopped writing and taking pictures. In fact, Villiers wrote more than forty books related to sailing and the sea, as well as some books for children.

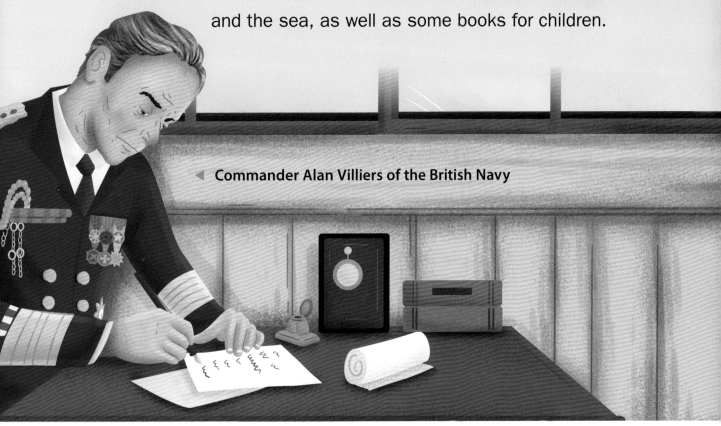

◀ **Commander Alan Villiers of the British Navy**

fortunate lucky

▶ **Before You Continue**

1. **Main Idea** Why were Villiers's writing and photographs important?
2. **Make Inferences** Why do you think the author says that serving in the navy was a "different type of adventure?"

Pearl Farming Today

The pearl industry in the Middle East **declined** in the 1930s, as Japan found a way to **ensure** that oysters created pearls. This made Japanese pearls much cheaper. Then, with the **expansion** of the oil industry, pearl diving in the Middle East disappeared completely.

Today, however, pearl farming has returned to the Gulf. Pollution in the seas has caused Japanese pearl production to decline, so, at the beginning of the 21st century, the Middle East's first pearl farm was opened. The owner of that farm, Mohamed al Suwaidi, remembered how the pearl divers of his grandfather's generation suffered. He wanted something better.

▲ A worker puts a bead into an oyster to create a pearl.

▲ Around eighty percent of cultured oysters produce pearls.

declined was greatly reduced
ensure make certain
expansion growth

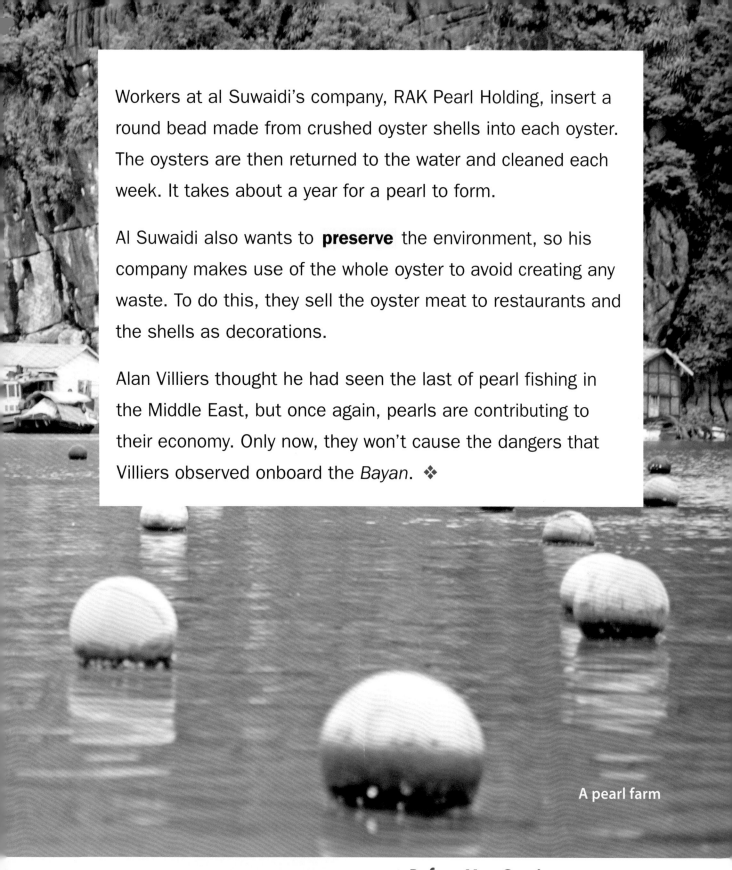

Workers at al Suwaidi's company, RAK Pearl Holding, insert a round bead made from crushed oyster shells into each oyster. The oysters are then returned to the water and cleaned each week. It takes about a year for a pearl to form.

Al Suwaidi also wants to **preserve** the environment, so his company makes use of the whole oyster to avoid creating any waste. To do this, they sell the oyster meat to restaurants and the shells as decorations.

Alan Villiers thought he had seen the last of pearl fishing in the Middle East, but once again, pearls are contributing to their economy. Only now, they won't cause the dangers that Villiers observed onboard the *Bayan*. ❖

A pearl farm

▶ **Before You Continue**

1. **Details** What does RAK Pearl Holding do with all the parts of the oyster?

2. **Sequence** How does the company make sure a pearl forms in the oyster? In what order are the steps performed?

Think and Respond

Key Words

archaeologist	galleon
artifact	merchant
colony	preserve
currency	route
examine	trade

Talk About It

1. What facts about people and events are in the **history article**? Give three examples.

2. Suppose you are telling a friend about the *Bayan*. **Restate an idea** that you learned about this ship.

From _____ , I know _____ . In other words, _____ .

3. Pretend you are reading Alan Villiers's book, "Sons of Sindbad." Tell a partner what information about pearl diving surprised you.

I just read about _____ . It surprised me because _____ .

Write About It

People often find adventures at sea exciting. However, they may dislike the fact that people lived in very difficult conditions. Decide what you think about life at sea for a Middle Eastern pearl diver in the 1930s. Then write a short essay to persuade readers to agree with you. Use **Key Words** to help you.

I *believe* that life at sea for pearl divers was _____ .
I *say* that *because of* _____ and _____ . I think you
will agree with me because _____ .

Sequence

Make a timeline for Alan Villier's life based on "Diving for Treasure." Put the events in the order they happened.

Timeline

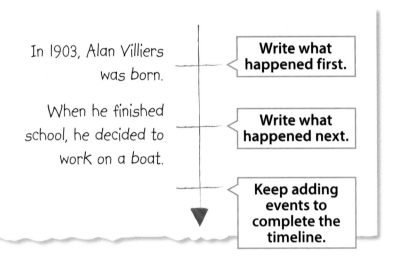

In 1903, Alan Villiers was born.

When he finished school, he decided to work on a boat.

Write what happened first.

Write what happened next.

Keep adding events to complete the timeline.

Now use your timeline as you retell "Diving for Treasure" to a partner. Use dates, time-order words, and **Key Words**.

In 1903, _____ .

Fluency

Practice reading with phrasing. Rate your reading.

Talk Together

Choose an illustration or photograph from "Diving for Treasure." Use **Key Words** as you tell a partner what the picture shows about searching for treasure at sea.

Suffixes

A suffix is a word part that comes at the end of a word.
It changes the meaning of the word.

The suffix **-er** often means "a person who does something."

trade + -er = trader

A **trader** is a person who trades.

Suffix	Origin	Meaning	Example
-al	Latin	belonging to	personal
-ation	Latin	act or process	preservation
-ist	Greek	a person who studies	archaeologist
-ly	Middle English	in a certain way	quickly

Try It Together

Read the sentences. Use the chart above to answer the questions.

The geologist broke up the rocks and held a stone. At first, he thought
it was just a plain rock. On closer examination, he saw a diamond.

1. **What is the work of a geologist?**

   A to crush stones

   B to find diamonds

   C to study rocks

   D to help archaeologists

2. **What does examination mean?**

   A the act of looking

   B the act of finding

   C to look closely

   D a person who finds things

La Belle Shipwreck

https://eltngl.com/reachhigherseries

La Belle Shipwreck

About • Special Exhibits • Prehistoric • Kids • Teachers • Resources Search ▶

Main

Explore the Shipwreck

Treasures of the *Belle*

ADAPTED FROM THE **TEXAS BEYOND HISTORY** WEBSITE

On a winter day in 1687, the French ship *Belle* **ran aground** off the coast of what is now the U.S. state of Texas. The ship was part of an **expedition** led by French explorer René-Robert Cavelier, Sieur de La Salle. La Salle had come to **establish** a French **colony**. The colony would have been a **base for invading** Mexico, which was controlled by Spain. France and Spain were then at war.

▲ René-Robert Cavelier, Sieur de La Salle (1643–1687)

NEXT ››

ran aground got stuck in land
expedition exploration journey
establish start
base for invading place to prepare for war against

▶ **Before You Continue**
1. **Predict** What do you think the main idea or topic of this selection will be?
2. **Use Text Features** Which link in the web article would you click to learn about gold and silver found aboard the *Belle*?

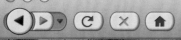

About • Special Exhibits • Prehistoric • Kids • Teachers • Resources

Search ▶

Main

Explore the
Shipwreck

Treasures
of the *Belle*

La Belle Shipwreck
PAGE [2] OF 3

≪ PREVIOUS | NEXT ≫

The First Expedition

This was not La Salle's first journey to the New World. In 1669 he set out to explore the Great Lakes region of North America. By 1682 he reached Illinois, establishing trading posts along the way.

La Salle's first expedition was a great success. He had claimed about one-third of the land in today's continental United States. He did so in the name of Louis XIV, King of France.

Now La Salle hoped to **conquer** even more **territory**, including the Spanish silver mines in northern Mexico.

▲ A painting showing La Salle naming the country "Louisiana"

▲ La Salle claimed about one-third of the continental United States for France.

conquer take control of
territory land

▲ Painting by Theodore Gudin titled *La Salle's Expedition to Louisiana in 1684*

Headed for Disaster

La Salle set sail from the French port of La Rochelle. The *Belle* was one of four ships in the expedition.

When the expedition reached the Caribbean Sea, it had its first piece of bad luck. Pirates seized one of the ships.

In January 1685, the remaining three ships reached a bay on the Texas coast by mistake. Then La Salle had more bad luck: One of the ships sank. Then another had to return to France. Only the *Belle* was left.

ZOOM

▲ This page from the journal of the *Belle*, dated January 17, 1685, describes what happened on the ship that day.

《 PREVIOUS | NEXT 》

▶ Before You Continue

1. **Details** What was the purpose of La Salle's new expedition?

2. **Make Inferences** Look at the journal entry and the caption. How might this journal help **archaeologists** learn more about the *Belle*?

About • Special Exhibits • Prehistoric • Kids • Teachers • Resources   Search ▶

La Belle Shipwreck

The Wreck

La Salle left the *Belle* to explore on foot, leaving his sailors in charge of the ship. The *Belle* was not **anchored well**. The sailors were tired and sick.

One day a fierce wind began to push the *Belle* across the bay. The crew could not manage the sails.

The heavy anchor dragged along the bottom of the bay until the ship hit a sandy **reef**. The reef wrecked the *Belle*, which gradually sank into the mud. The *Belle* remained buried for 310 years, untouched but not forgotten.

The *Belle*'s crew tried to save supplies from the wrecked ship. ▶

anchored well held safely in place

reef a ridge of jagged rock, coral, or sand

The Discovery

Archaeologists from the Texas Historical Commission finally found the *Belle* in 1995. They discovered one of the *Belle* cannons, which **confirmed** the identity of the wreck.

▲ Texas archaeologists slowly uncovered the *Belle*.

Most of the ship's contents were found in good condition. Wooden boxes were **jammed** with goods to **trade**, tools, rope, dishes—everything needed to establish a **colony** in the New World.

The story of the *Belle* did not end there. The French government claimed that the shipwreck and all its contents belonged to France. In 2003 the French and the American governments signed **a treaty**. France now owns the *Belle*, but the Texas Historical Commission takes care of the ship. ❖

▲ Archaeologists have found more than one million **artifacts** from the *Belle*.

≪ PREVIOUS

---

confirmed proved
jammed filled
a treaty an agreement

▶ **Before You Continue**
1. **Cause/Effect** Why did the *Belle* sink?
2. **Clarify** How did **archaeologists** know they had found the *Belle*?

Key Words

archaeologist	galleon
artifact	merchant
colony	preserve
currency	route
examine	trade

Compare Media Texts

"La Belle Shipwreck" is an example of a web article. A blog is another form of writing on the Internet. Find an example of a blog. Compare it with "La Belle Shipwreck." Complete a comparison chart.

Comparison Chart

Feature	Web article	Blog
Title	"La Belle Shipwreck"	
Source of information	Texas Beyond History	
Date when written?	no	
Is the text in sections?		
Are there pictures?		
Does the information change often?		
Are there mostly facts or mostly opinions?		
Are there links to other articles and websites or definitions?		

Talk Together

Why do **archaeologists** and explorers seek treasure? Think about the two articles. Use Key Words to talk about your ideas.

Possessive Pronouns

Possessive pronouns tell who or what owns something. Be sure to use the correct pronoun.

Grammar Rules Possessive Pronouns

• For yourself, use **mine**.	The treasures are **mine**.
• For yourself and one or more persons, use **ours**.	That ship is **ours**.
• When you speak to one or more persons, use **yours**.	These objects are **yours**.
• For one other person or thing, use **his** or **hers**.	Are those coins **his**? No, I think they are **hers**.
• For two or more persons or things, use **theirs**.	The ship with the tall sails is **theirs**.

Read Pronouns

Read the sentences. Find two possessive pronouns.

The captain kept the pearls. They weren't his though because he had to sell them to merchants. The pearls weren't theirs either. They sold them to master jewelers.

Write Pronouns

Imagine that you are exploring a shipwreck. Write a journal entry about what you and the other workers find one day. Use at least two possessive pronouns.

Write as a Storyteller

Write Historical Fiction

Write an adventure story that takes place before steamships replaced sailboats. You will share your story during a storytelling festival.

Study a Model

Historical fiction is a story that is set in the past. Read Brandon's story about Haamid Nazari, the boy sailor.

The beginning introduces the **characters** and **setting** and gives details.

Sailor Boy

by Brandon Kelly

I had never thought about sailing. But then **Father's** friend, **Alan Villiers**, invited us to join him for a journey on **the good ship *Bayan*** and my adventure began.

Our voyage on the dhow lasted four months. When we set out in mid-May I was frightened. But my fear soon changed to excitement.

At night, I listened to the pearl divers tell stories about the adventures they'd had and the treasures they hoped to find at the bottom of the sea. One diver had found five pearls in one day! Finally, I went up to the captain himself.

"Captain al-Nejdi," I said. "I want to join the crew."

The captain laughed. **"Well, well. Young Master Haamid Nazari, is it? And what if I say no?"**

"Then I will jump into the sea," I said.

The captain stopped laughing. And I became a sailor.

The story stays focused on one event. The **dialogue**, or what the characters say, may sound the way people spoke long ago.

Prewrite

1. **Choose a Topic** What time and place will you choose for your story? Talk with a partner to find fun ideas.

> ### Language Frames
>
> | **Tell Your Ideas** | **Respond to Ideas** |
> |---|---|
> | • I'd love to write a story where someone _____. | • Do you know a lot about _____? |
> | • My favorite historical character is _____. | • Where will you find details about _____? |

2. **Gather Information** For historical fiction, you have to do research. Find the details you need to describe your characters and setting accurately.

3. **Get Organized** Think about the main character in your story. How will the character change? What events and relationships will bring about the changes? Use a character map to plan.

Character Map

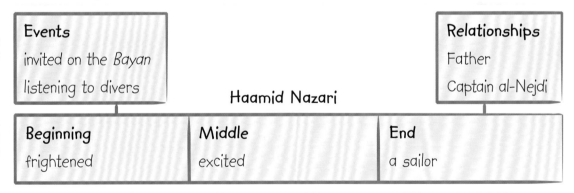

Draft

Use your character map and the details you found to write your draft.

- Make sure each event flows logically to the next.

- Use your research to describe your setting and characters accurately.

Revise

1. **Read, Retell, Respond** Read your draft aloud to a partner. Your partner listens and then retells the story. Next, talk about ways to improve your writing.

Language Frames

Retell	Make Suggestions
• Your story was about _____ .	• I don't understand why _____ .
• The story took place in _____ .	• I can't really picture _____ . Can you add more details?
• Your main characters were _____ .	• Your characters don't seem like _____ . What if you _____ ?

---

2. **Make Changes** Think about your draft and your partner's suggestions. Use revision marks to make your changes.

- Is your story accurate? Check all of your details.

> One diver had found ~~fifty~~ five pearls in one day!

- Make sure your story is focused. Remove details that don't add to the story.

> When we set out in mid-May I was frightened. ~~I had never been sailing before and I didn't know what to expect.~~ But my fear soon changed to excitement.

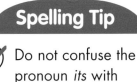

Spelling Tip

Do not confuse the pronoun *its* with the contraction *it's*.

Edit and Proofread

Work with a partner to edit and proofread your story.
Make sure you use pronouns correctly.

Present

On Your Own Make a final copy of your story. Choose a way to share it with your classmates. You can read it aloud, or give it to someone else to read.

Presentation Tips	
If you are the speaker...	**If you are the listener...**
Before you read, practice saying any historical names or terms you may have used.	Connect the story with what you already know about the time period.
Try to listen to yourself read. Adjust your pitch, volume, or speed if you need to.	Listen for details that help you picture the time and place.

In a Group Hold a storytelling festival. Memorize your story, and practice telling it with gestures and emotion. Dress in a costume that matches the time period. Present your stories to other classes, or invite younger children to hear them.

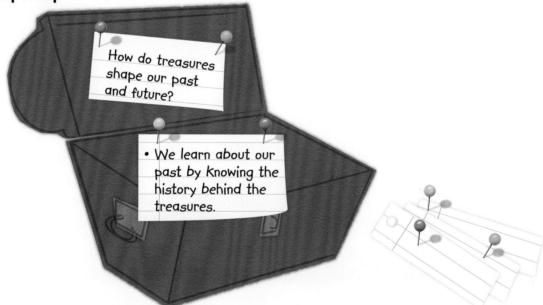

BIG Question

How do treasures shape our past and future?

In this unit, you found lots of answers to the **Big Question**. Now use your concept map to discuss the **Big Question** with the class.

Concept Map

How do treasures shape our past and future?

• We learn about our past by knowing the history behind the treasures.

Write a Song

Choose one reason that people seek treasure. Write the lyrics, or words, for a song that describes the reason in detail. You may want to choose the tune first.

Share Your Ideas

Choose one of these ways to share your ideas about the **Big Question**.

Write It!

Make a Comic Book

Form a comic book with eight blank pages. Then plan a story about an explorer or a sailor. Draw pictures to tell the story. Use captions to explain the events. Share your comic book with the class.

Talk About It!

Talk Show

Choose people to represent adventurers such as René-Robert Cavelier. Host a talk show. Ask each adventurer to tell about seeking treasure.

Do It!

Make a Time Capsule

Have everyone in the class bring in one artifact to put in a time capsule. It should be something you can live without for now. Decide when you will open the time capsule in the future. What would people discover about your class?

Write It!

Write a Sailor's Journal

Write a journal entry as though you are a sailor on a boat in a time before steamships ruled the sea.

Unit 7

MOVING THROUGH SPACE

What does it take to explore space?

INTERNATIONAL SPACE STATION
An astronaut making some repairs on the outside of the station during a spacewalk

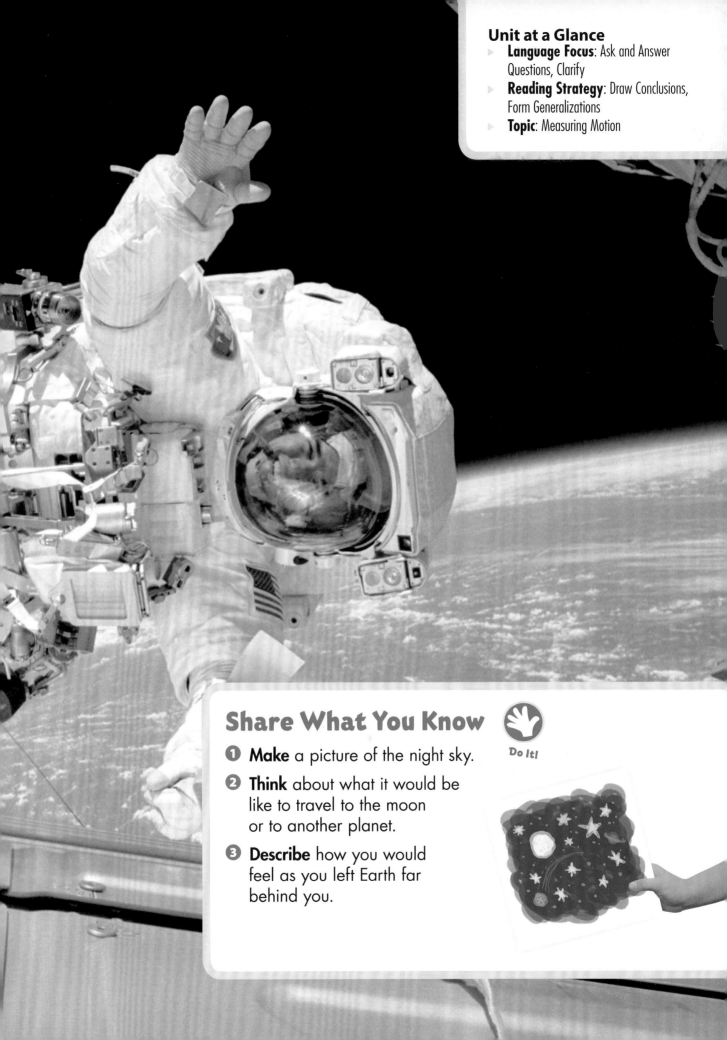

Share What You Know

Do It!

1. **Make** a picture of the night sky.

2. **Think** about what it would be like to travel to the moon or to another planet.

3. **Describe** how you would feel as you left Earth far behind you.

Ask and Answer Questions

Listen to the dialogue between Binh and Sofia. Then use **Language Frames** to ask and answer questions with a partner. Talk about objects in space that you wonder about.

Language Frames

- When is _____ ?
- It's _____ .
- Where are _____ ?
- They're _____ .

Dialogue

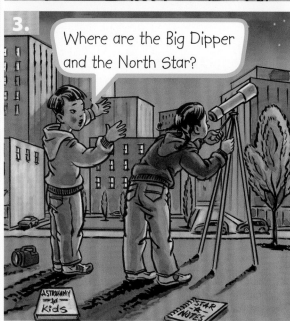

🔊 Key Words

Look at the pictures. Use **Key Words** and other words to talk about how **motion** makes sports exciting.

Key Words
accelerate
height
measure
motion
speed

Exciting Sports Moments

Listen to the engines roar! The cars **accelerate** quickly to well over 100 miles per hour!

Look at the **height** of that player's jump! He makes touching the rim look easy!

Look at her strong legs! This track star can move at top **speed**.

The fans wait for the officials to **measure**. How far did a player move the ball?

Talk Together

What are some ways to measure how we move through space? Try to use **Language Frames** from page 146 and **Key Words** to ask and answer questions about this topic with a partner.

Compare and Contrast

When you **compare** things, you say how they are similar, or alike.
When you **contrast** them, you say how they are different.

Look at the pictures of Earth and Mars. Read the text.

Earth has a diameter of 13,000 kilometers (8,078 miles). It is 150 million kilometers (93 million miles) from the sun.

Mars has a diameter of 6,800 kilometers (4,225 miles). It is 228 million kilometers (142 million miles) from the sun.

Map and Talk

You can use a comparison chart to show how two things are alike and different. Here's how to make one.

Comparison Chart

Planet	Diameter	Distance from Sun	Characteristics
Earth	13,000 Kilometers (8,078 miles)	150 million Kilometers	looks blue and green has living things
Mars	6,800 Kilometers (4,225 miles)	228 million Kilometers	looks red has no living things

Write headings here.

Give information in these rows.

Talk Together

Look back at page 147. Choose another sport that requires speed and strength. Compare it to one of the sports shown. Make a comparison chart with a partner.

🔊 More Key Words

Use these words to talk about "What's Faster than a Speeding Cheetah?" and "Building for Space Travel."

average
noun

An **average** is an amount that is usual for a group. Bears have an **average** of two cubs.

distance
noun

Distance is the amount of space between things. Today, we can fly a long **distance** very quickly.

rate
noun

The **rate** of an action is its speed. Turtles move at a slow **rate**.

scale
noun

1"=1 mile

A **scale** gives size comparisons. The **scale** of this map shows that 1 inch is equal to 1 mile.

solve
verb

To **solve** a problem means to figure it out. When you **solve** a puzzle, it's done.

Talk Together

Work with a partner. For each **Key Word**, write a sentence that shows what the word means.

I am going to _solve_ a math problem.

Learn to Draw Conclusions

Look at the picture. What do Binh and Sofia plan to do? Look for details. Put the information together to **draw a conclusion**, or decide, what they will do.

You also **draw conclusions** when you read.

How to Draw Conclusions

1. Notice an important idea in the text.

2. Look for another idea that you think is important.

3. How do the ideas go with one another? Put the ideas together to draw a conclusion.

I read _____.

I also read _____.

I connect the ideas and conclude _____.

Language Frames

👁 I read _____ .

👁 I also read
_____ .

🧩 I connect the
ideas and
conclude _____ .

Talk **Together**

Read Binh's book report. Read the sample
conclusion. Draw your own conclusions. Then use
Language Frames to tell a partner about them.

Book Report

All About *All About Io*

by Binh Pham

Do you want to know more about the crazy world of outer
space? If so, you should read *All About Io* by Jin Park. It is full of
interesting facts about Jupiter.

I learned that Jupiter has 63 moons! A lot of them started out
as asteroids. Then they got too close to Jupiter, which has a huge
mass. That means it also has a lot of gravity. Think about the
difference in **scale**: Jupiter is huge, the asteroids are tiny. They
got trapped by Jupiter's gravity. Now they orbit Jupiter.

At first, the title of the book confused me. Reading it **solved**
the puzzle for me. Io is one of Jupiter's largest moons. It is
covered with volcanoes that erupt. The explosions color the moon with
yellows and oranges, but I wouldn't want to live there.

The book gives lots of information. It tells how to estimate how
much you would weigh on Jupiter. I also learned that Jupiter rotates at
a faster **rate** than any other planet in our solar system. On **average**,
a day on Jupiter lasts just 9 hours and 55 minutes. Getting to Jupiter
would take a very long time, even for the fastest modern space ship.
The **distance** between the two planets is about 390 million miles.

This book was so much fun to read. I will look for more books by
Park when I go to the library.

Sample Conclusion

"I read that this book
has a lot of facts.

I also read that it is
about the real planet
Jupiter.

I connect the ideas and
conclude the book is
nonfiction. It does not
tell a story the author
made up."

◀ = A good place to draw a conclusion

Read a Math Article

Genre

A **math article** is nonfiction. It gives number facts about people, places, or events.

Text Feature

Graphs show data, or information that uses numbers. A **bar graph** is one kind of graph. Each bar represents one piece of information.

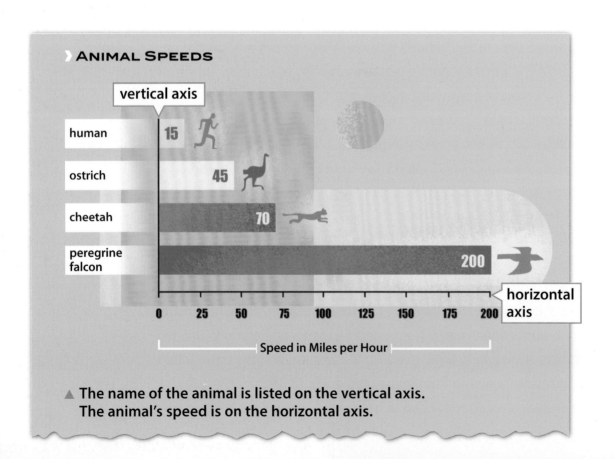

❯ ANIMAL SPEEDS

vertical axis

human	15
ostrich	45
cheetah	70
peregrine falcon	200

0 25 50 75 100 125 150 175 200   horizontal axis

Speed in Miles per Hour

▲ The name of the animal is listed on the vertical axis. The animal's speed is on the horizontal axis.

WHAT'S FASTER THAN A SPEEDING CHEETAH?

>>> by Robert E. Wells

▶ Set a Purpose
Learn about the **speeds** of different
animals and objects in our universe.

How Fast Is Fast?

You may be **fast on your feet**, but if you want to win races,
never race a cheetah, or even an ostrich, for that matter.

If you ran very hard, you might reach a **speed** of 24 kilometers
(15 miles) per hour. That's not nearly fast enough to keep up
with an ostrich.

An ostrich is the world's fastest two-legged runner. It has a top
speed of about 72 kilometers (45 miles) per hour. In a race
though, the cheetah would certainly be **way out in front**.

▲ **A peregrine falcon in downward
flight is faster than any animal
that lives on land.**

fast on your feet
a great runner

way out in front first

A cheetah can reach a **speed** of about 113 kilometers (70 miles) per hour. That's more than a mile a minute. No animal on Earth can run faster than that.

But a cheetah can't run as fast as a peregrine falcon can **swoop**.

A peregrine falcon can dive through the sky at about 322 kilometers (200 miles) per hour. That's three times as fast as a car **zooming** along a highway.

A peregrine falcon is magnificent. It can dive faster than any creature can run. But it can't fly as fast as an airplane.

▶ ANIMAL SPEEDS

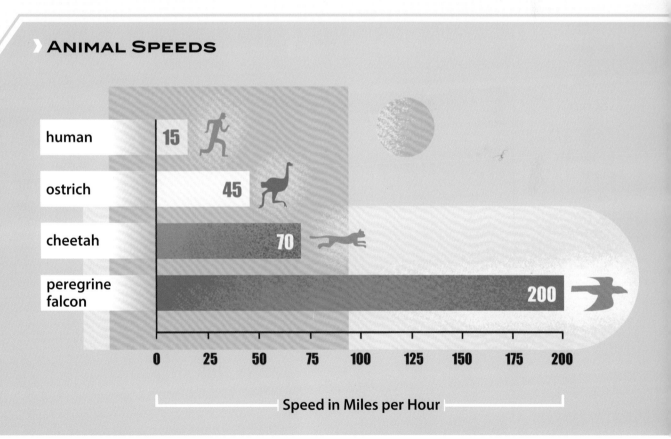

Speed in Miles per Hour

swoop fly downward
zooming traveling at a fast speed

▶ Before You Continue
1. **Compare/Contrast** How much faster than a person can an ostrich run?
2. **Ask Questions** What is one question you have about the information in the graph?

Flight Times

Some propeller planes can fly more than 483 kilometers (300 miles) per hour. With a **propeller** pulling you through the air, you can travel faster than the fastest falcon.

With a jet engine, you can fly faster than the fastest propeller plane. In fact, you can fly even faster than the **speed** of sound.

Sound travels in waves. **At high altitudes**, where jets fly, sound waves travel about 1,062 kilometers (660 miles) per hour. Some very fast jets can fly twice the speed of sound.

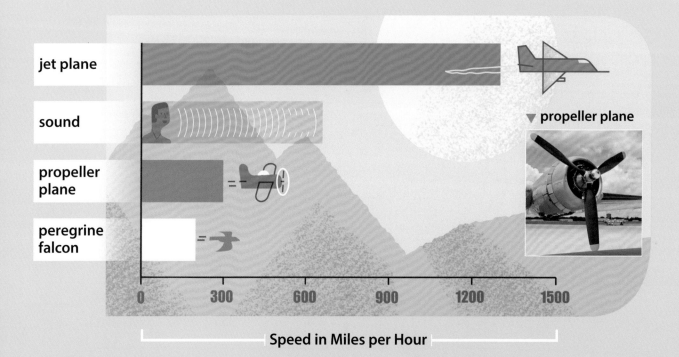

jet plane	
sound	
propeller plane	
peregrine falcon	

▼ propeller plane

0   300   600   900   1200   1500

Speed in Miles per Hour

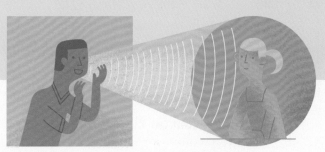

▲ **Sound waves travel through the air.**

propeller a device with spinning blades that helps a plane move

At high altitudes High in the air; Miles above the ground

If you shouted to someone who was traveling faster than sound, your voice would not go fast enough to catch up to him or her. The person would never hear you.

Faster Still

If you want to travel to the moon, you're going to need something that's much faster than a jet. You'll need a rocket ship.

To escape Earth's **gravity** and travel into space, a rocket ship must go faster than any jet. To travel to the moon, a rocket ship must reach a **speed** of about 40,234 kilometers (25,000 miles) per hour. That's more than thirty times as fast as sound.

A rocket ship takes off with incredible speed.

gravity the natural force that causes things to fall toward the Earth

▶ Before You Continue

1. **Compare/Contrast** Compare the **speed** of a jet with the speed of sound. Which travels faster?

2. **Explain** In your own words, explain why a rocket needs to go faster than a jet.

You can turn off your rockets and **coast** after you're in space. That's because there's little to no drag in space. *Drag* is a force that acts against objects when they travel through air. Drag slows down moving objects. Now, speeding through space at 40,234 kilometers (25,000 miles) per hour is **mighty** fast.

What's that zooming by, going so much faster that you feel like you are standing still? It's a meteoroid!

A meteoroid is a space rock. Some meteoroids **streak** through space at 241,402 kilometers (150,000 miles) per hour. That's six times faster than your rocket ship is traveling.

❯ DRAG ON A BALL

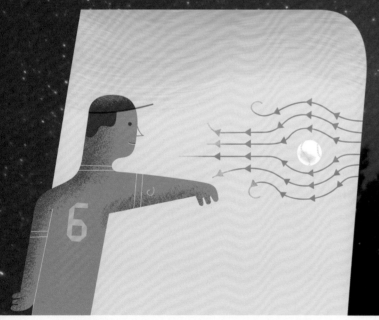

meteoroid

▲ The ball pushes against the air as it travels. Air pushes back. The ball slows down.

coast keep moving without using additional power

mighty very

streak zoom; move

As you circle around the moon and head back to Earth, you might be thinking that the meteoroid you saw was the fastest thing you could ever see.

FASTER AND FASTER

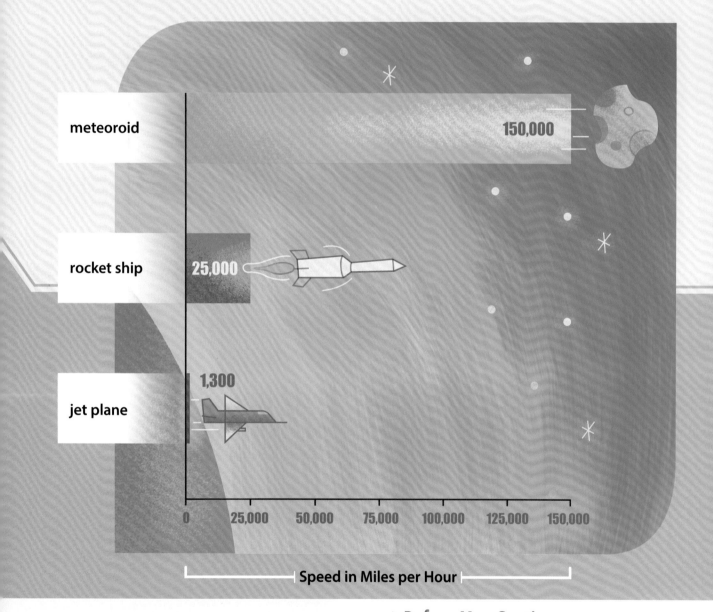

meteoroid — 150,000

rocket ship — 25,000

jet plane — 1,300

0   25,000   50,000   75,000   100,000   125,000   150,000

Speed in Miles per Hour

▶ Before You Continue

1. **Draw Conclusions** What can you conclude about why meteoroids can travel so fast in space?

2. **Use Text Features** What does the bar graph on this page compare?

Fastest of All

Hold on a minute. There's something much faster than even the fastest meteoroid. It's something you see all the time.

Just push the switch on a flashlight. Instantly, a light beam will flash out at the amazing **speed** of 299,338 kilometers (186,000 miles) per second.

That's thousands of times faster than a meteoroid. At that speed, a beam of light could circle Earth more than seven times in one second.

186,000 miles per second

Hold on Wait

Most scientists believe that nothing can travel through space faster than light. Who would have thought that the fastest traveling thing in the whole universe could come out of something small enough to hold in your hand?

◄ A beam of light could circle Earth more than seven times in one second!

HOW LONG WOULD IT TAKE TO TRAVEL FROM EARTH TO THE MOON (239,000 MILES)?

AT THIS SPEED...	IT WOULD TAKE ABOUT
Young Runner (15 miles per hour)	1 ¾ years
Ostrich (45 miles per hour)	7 ⅓ months
Cheetah (70 miles per hour)	4 ⅔ months
Peregrine Falcon (200 miles per hour)	7 weeks
Propeller Plane (300 miles per hour)	4 ⅔ weeks
Supersonic Jet (1,400 miles per hour)	1 week
Rocket Ship (25,000 miles per hour)	9 ½ hours
Meteoroid (150,000 miles per hour)	1 ½ hours
Light (186,000 miles per second)	1 ⅓ seconds

▶ Before You Continue

1. **Draw Conclusions** What detail supports the conclusion that a light beam travels faster than a meteoroid?

2. **Interpret** Based on the chart, which three objects travel fastest though space?

Some Additional Thoughts on Very Fast Things

Sometimes **speeds** are hard to **measure**. People often have trouble measuring the speeds of animals. The numbers in this article are the best estimates. It would be much simpler if cheetahs, ostriches, and falcons **came with** speedometers.

The speed of sound through air is easier to measure than the speeds of wild animals. Still, the speed of sound **is not constant**. It's about 1,223 kilometers (760 miles) per hour at sea level. At high altitudes, where the air is thin and cold, it slows to about 1,062 kilometers (660 miles) per hour.

› SPEED OF SOUND AT HIGH AND LOW ALTITUDES

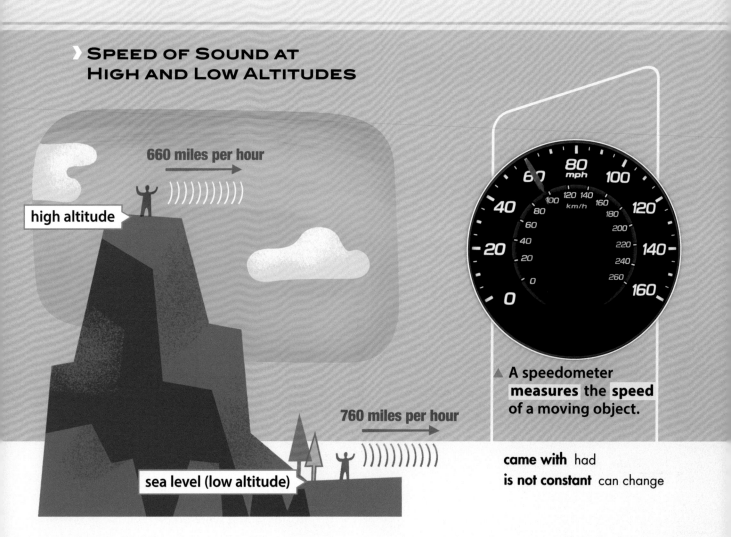

660 miles per hour

high altitude

sea level (low altitude)

760 miles per hour

▲ A speedometer **measures** the **speed** of a moving object.

came with had
is not constant can change

Meteoroids zoom through space at different **speeds**, too. The fastest meteoroids travel through the solar system at a speed of around 42 kilometers (26 miles) per second.

The amazing speed of light, traveling through space at 299,338 kilometers (186,000 miles) per second, is one of the few speeds that **is constant**.

Light beams flashing through space are usually shown as bright rays. A real light beam, however, becomes bright and visible only when it hits such things as dust or water particles.

Now you know what the fastest thing in the universe is. The next time you're in a conversation about speed, you'll be able to **shed some light on** the subject! ❖

is constant always stays the same
shed some light on explain

▶ **Before You Continue**

1. **Draw Conclusions** What makes the **speed** of sound easier to **measure** than a racing animal?

2. **Compare/Contrast** Describe one way in which the speed of light and the speed of sound are different.

163

Think and Respond

Key Words	
accelerate	motion
average	rate
distance	scale
height	solve
measure	speed

Talk About It

1. How can you use the graphs in this **math article** to compare and contrast moving objects?

2. How does the **speed** of sound compare to the speed of light? With a partner, **ask and answer questions** about this topic.

   Is _____ faster than _____?

   Yes, _____ travels _____, and _____ travels _____.

3. The author says that researchers have to estimate how fast animals move. Summarize what it means to estimate the speed of a moving object.

   When you estimate, you _____. Researchers have to estimate animal speeds because _____.

Write About It

Who is the fastest runner in your class? Write a set of instructions for a race. In your instructions, tell how you would **measure** each person's running speed. Also tell what kind of graph you would use to compare the **rates**. Use **Key Words** in your list.

1. Mark the starting line of the race.
2. Mark the _____.

Compare and Contrast

Make a comparison chart for "What's Faster Than a Speeding Cheetah?"

In this column, name the things you will compare.

Tell how it moves.

Tell how fast it is.

Tell what speed record it set.

Animal or Object	How It Moves	Fastest Speed	Record
ostrich	runs on two legs	72 km (45 mi) per hour	fastest animal with 2 legs
cheetah	runs on four legs	113 km (70 mi) per hour	fastest land animal
peregrine falcon			
propeller plane			

Now use your comparison chart as you tell a partner how the animals and objects are alike and how they are different. Use **Key Words** and words like *but* and *however* to compare.

A _____ is fast, but a _____ is faster.

Fluency

Practice reading with intonation. Rate your reading.

Talk Together

Why do we need to be fast to explore space? Use **Key Words** as you talk about space exploration and **motion**.

Multiple-Meaning Words

Some words have more than one meaning. You can use context to figure out the correct meaning.

Rate is a **multiple-meaning word**. In the sentence below, **rate** means *speed*. You can use the words *travels* and *slower* as clues to the meaning.

> The **rate** at which sound travels is slower where the air is thin and cold.

> **rate** *noun* **1.** the speed at which something moves **2.** a fee charged for a service

Try It Together

Read the passage. Then answer the questions.

> Just push the **switch** on a flashlight. Instantly, a **beam** will flash out at the amazing speed of 299,338 kilometers (186,000 miles) per second.

1. **What is the best definition for beam in this passage?**

   A a long piece of wood or metal

   B the widest part of a ship

   C the bar on a balance scale

   D a ray of light

2. **What is the best definition for switch in this passage?**

   A a section of railroad track

   B an on/off button

   C a change

   D a fast, jerking motion

Making Connections You read a math article about the **speed** of moving objects such as space ships. Now read a report about designing a spacecraft.

Genre A **science report** presents facts about a topic. Most reports have a title and an introduction that tells what the report is about. Often, a conclusion sums up the report.

Building for
SPACE TRAVEL

by Anastasia Suen

Imagine this task: Design a space **vehicle** that will also be a home for astronauts on a **mission** to planet Mars that could take months or years. For **architect** Constance Adams, this job was tough. She designed TransHab—a "transit habitat" where astronauts would live and work. Not surprisingly, Adams faced many challenges along the way.

Earth

Mars

Sun

vehicle craft
mission trip
architect building designer

▶ **Before You Continue**

1. **Make Connections** Think about the length of time for this mission. What do you think the TransHab might need?

2. **Make Predictions** What design challenges do you think Adams faced?

NASA did not expect TransHab to launch into space on its own. A space shuttle was supposed to carry it into space. So TransHab had to be small enough to fit inside a shuttle's **cargo** area, and big enough for six astronauts to live in.

How would this be possible? Think about a beach ball. It's flat until you fill it with air. NASA asked Adams to use this idea for TransHab. Therefore, Adams had to design TransHab so it could be carried into space in its flattened state. Once it was in space, TransHab would be **inflated**.

cargo area

◀ A space shuttle was supposed to carry TransHab into space.

cargo storage
inflated filled with air

TransHab's soft outer surface created safety challenges. Space is a very dangerous place. Chunks of ice and rock **speed** along at four miles a second. Some types of **radiation**, or energy traveling through space, can also hurt astronauts' bodies. Most spacecraft have a hard outside shell to protect it from damage and keep radiation out.

Adams's team had to figure out how strong TransHab's soft outer shell needed to be. They made a one-foot-thick skin that combined different materials. One very strong material was Kevlar, which is used in convertible cars.

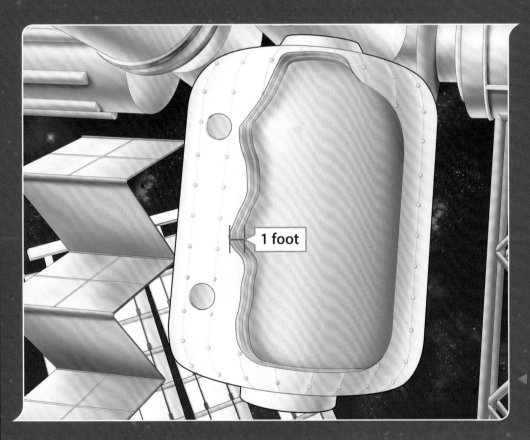

1 foot

◄ TransHab's outer skin is one foot thick.

radiation energy that moves from one place to another

▶ Before You Continue

1. **Draw Conclusions** Based on the text, what can you conclude about the risks of space travel?

2. **Compare/Contrast** How is TransHab different from a traditional spacecraft?

A trip to Mars would take a long time. Astronauts would have to live inside TransHab for years. They would need a real home in space. They would need places to eat, sleep, exercise, get care when sick, and have **privacy**. They would also need a group area for meetings and for celebrating special occasions like birthdays.

"We had to create a design for long-term living," Adams explained.

The diagram below shows Adams's plan for TransHab. There are three levels with living areas. The top level is a tunnel entryway and exit.

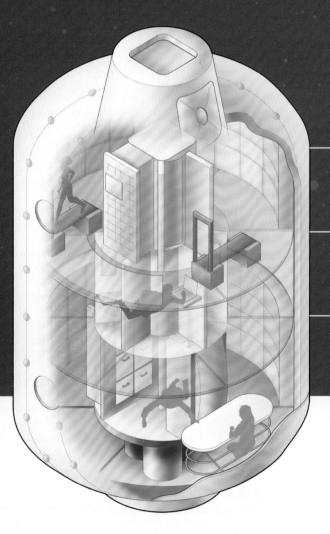

Level Four:
Entry and Exit Tunnel

Level Three:
Exercise Room, Bathroom, and Storage

Level Two:
Control Room and Six Bedrooms

Level One:
Kitchen and Dining Room

privacy space to be alone

Gravity is the force that keeps you firmly on the ground. Other forces of **motion** can cancel out the force of gravity. This creates a condition called *zero gravity*. A zero-gravity environment presents a design challenge because it causes objects to "float."

Adams attached furniture and other objects **securely** inside TransHab so astronauts could grab them to help themselves move around. She also used a pattern on the walls to help the astronauts tell up from down.

After years of hard work, Constance Adams met all these challenges. However, space scientists must meet other challenges before they can launch a mission to Mars. Even if TransHab does not go to Mars, it could be a home for astronauts on a future **space station**. ❖

▲ **An astronaut in zero gravity**

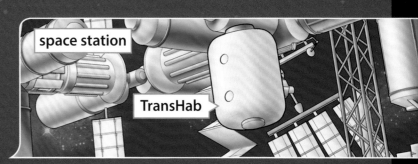

▲ **TransHab on a space station**

securely firmly

space station ship in space
  where astronauts work

▶ Before You Continue

1. **Use Text Features** Look at the diagram on page 170. Describe the areas that make TransHab a real home for astronauts.

2. **Draw Conclusions** What can you conclude about zero gravity's effects on astronauts?

Key Words

accelerate	motion
average	rate
distance	scale
height	solve
measure	speed

Compare Fact and Opinion

A **fact** is a statement that can be proved true. An **opinion** tells what someone thinks, feels, or believes. An author may include both facts and opinions, even in a nonfiction text. Work with a partner to complete the comparison chart. Discuss how you can tell if a statement is fact or opinion.

Write statements of fact in this column.

In this column, write statements that express opinions.

Comparison Chart

	Facts	Opinions
"What's Faster Than a Speeding Cheetah?"		A peregrine falcon is magnificent.
"Building for Space Travel"	Constance Adams helped design TransHab.	

Talk Together

Think about the math article and the science report. Use **Key Words** to discuss what it takes to explore space. Speak clearly and support your opinion.

Adverbs

Adverbs usually tell more about a verb.

Grammar Rules Adverbs

• Use an **adverb** to tell how, where, or when something happens.	An eagle flies **smoothly**. *(how)* It soars **upward**. *(where)* I watch an eagle **now**. *(when)*
• For some adverbs, add **-er** to compare two actions. Add **-est** to compare three or more actions.	A marlin swims fast**er** than a shark. A sailfish swims the fast**est** of all fish.
• If an adverb ends in **-ly**, use **more** or **less** to compare two actions. Use **the most** or **the least** to compare three or more actions.	Snakes move more gent**ly** than lizards. Lizards move less gent**ly** than snakes. Sloths move the most gent**ly** of all. Frogs move the least gent**ly** of all.

Read Adverbs

Read this passage with a partner. Find three adverbs.

If you shouted loudly and clearly to someone who was traveling faster than sound, the person would never hear you.

Write Adverbs

Write a paragraph about objects in motion, such as kites or paper airplanes. Share your paragraph with a partner. Use at least three adverbs.

Clarify

Listen to Francisco's song. Then use Language Frames to clarify information about the moon.

Song 🔊 ♪

LET'S GO TO THE MOON

Look up in the night for a circle that's bright.
Yes, it means you should look for the moon.
There are no creatures there—
    for example, no bears.
Let's all ride in a spaceship there soon.

Chorus
Let's go to the moon.
On our way we can all sing this tune.
If you want some more space,
    then the moon is the place.
We will have lots of room on the moon.

Tune: "Home on the Range"

BYE

BYE

MOON EXPRESS

BYE

Key Words
astronaut
launch
orbit
planet
rotation

🔊 Key Words

Look at the photos. Use **Key Words** and other words to talk about how you could teach younger children about space.

Tools for Teaching Very Young Children About Space

action figure astronaut As you talk about modern space travelers, let the children play with this astronaut. They can show the astronaut at work.

globe Use the globe as you teach children that Earth is a **planet**. Show them that planets are round. Demonstrate the Earth's **rotation**, or how it spins.

space shuttle model Tell children that many astronauts travel in the space shuttle. Demonstrate how the space shuttle **launches**, or takes off from Earth. Then use the model and the globe to show how the space shuttle **orbits**, or moves around, Earth.

solar system model Use the model as you tell children about the other planets in the solar system. Demonstrate how the planets orbit around the Sun.

Talk Together

What does it take for astronauts to explore space? Try to use **Language Frames** from page 174 and **Key Words** as you clarify your ideas with a partner.

Thinking Map

Plot

The action in a story is the **plot**. Every plot is built around a problem. When you follow the plot, you see:

- one event leads to the next event.

- at the turning point, an important change happens.

- at the solution, the problem is solved.

Look at the pictures. Follow the plot.

Map and Talk

You can use a plot diagram to retell a story. First, explain what the problem is. Then tell the events in the order they happen. Next, tell the turning point. Finally, explain how the problem is solved.

Plot Diagram

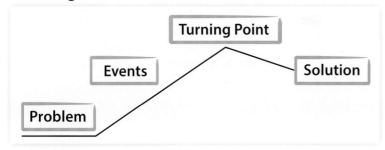

Problem: Francisco's rocket crash-lands.

Events: Francisco picks up the rocket. He sees that it is getting banged up.

Turning Point: Francisco and his dad make a parachute.

Solution: The rocket lands softly.

Talk Together

Use a plot diagram to explain one of your favorite stories. Then retell the story to a partner.

More Key Words

Use these words to talk about "The Moon Over Star" and "The First Person on the Moon."

capacity
noun

The **capacity** of an object is the most it can hold. This glass has a **capacity** of half a pint.

constant
noun

Something that never changes is a **constant**. The number of days in a week is a **constant**.

limit
verb

To **limit** something is to stop it after a a set amount of time. Many parents **limit** TV viewing.

resistance
noun

Resistance is a slowing force. Deep snow creates **resistance** when you walk in it.

technology
noun

Technology is the use of science to solve problems. Doctors rely on **technology**.

Talk Together

Work with a partner to complete a Meaning Map for each **Key Word**.

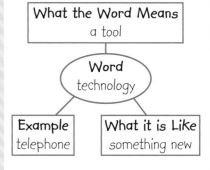

What the Word Means
a tool

Word
technology

Example
telephone

What it is Like
something new

177

Learn to Form Generalizations

Look at the photographs. Notice details that show what it takes to be a good **astronaut**. Think about what you already know about space travel.

From this information, you can **form a generalization** about what most astronauts have in common.

You also **form generalizations** when you read.

How to Form Generalizations

 1. As you read, think about the important ideas in the text.

I read _____.

 2. Think about how the ideas fit together with what you know or have experienced.

I know_____.

 3. Create a statement that seems true for both the text and what you know. Use words like *some, many, most,* or *all.*

Most of the time, it is true that _____.

Talk Together

Read Francisco's story. Read the sample generalization. Then use **Language Frames** to tell a partner about your own generalizations.

Story

Game Over

by Francisco Soto

Ramón gets what he wanted for his birthday: the brand new video game *Planet Surfer*. As soon as he starts playing, his little brother Nico wants to play, too. Ramón ignores him.

Ramón plays the character Zozo in *Planet Surfer*. Zozo is an explorer in outer space. He uses lots of amazing space **technology**.

The game is great, but Nico's nagging is a **constant**. When Zozo **launches** his rocket, Nico tugs on Ramón's arm. "Stop bothering me!" says Ramón, trying to **limit** his little brother's interruptions.

Zozo collects rock samples as he explores the **planets**. The ship is loaded down, near to **capacity**. He wants one more rock. Yes, it fits! Nico claps loudly. "Shhh," says Ramón.

Zozo overcomes a giant space robot. When the battle is over, Nico finally overcomes Ramón's **resistance**. Ramón gives Nico the controller and lets him play.

> **Sample Generalization**
>
> "I read that Ramón is playing a brand new game.
>
> I know I feel excited when I play a new game for the first time.
>
> Most of the time, it is true that people would like to play a new game without being interrupted."

◀ A good place to form a generalization

179

Read a Story

Genre

Realistic fiction tells a story about events that really happened or could happen. The characters and setting in this story seem real, but were created by the author.

Dialogue in a Story

The dialogue in a story is what the characters say. Quotation marks signal the beginning or the end of a character's speech. The words that appear between the quotation marks are the speaker's exact words.

quotation marks · dialogue · quotation marks

"I wonder how many miles it is to the moon," Cousin Carrie said. < the person speaking

I'd been reading the moon stories in the paper, so I knew.

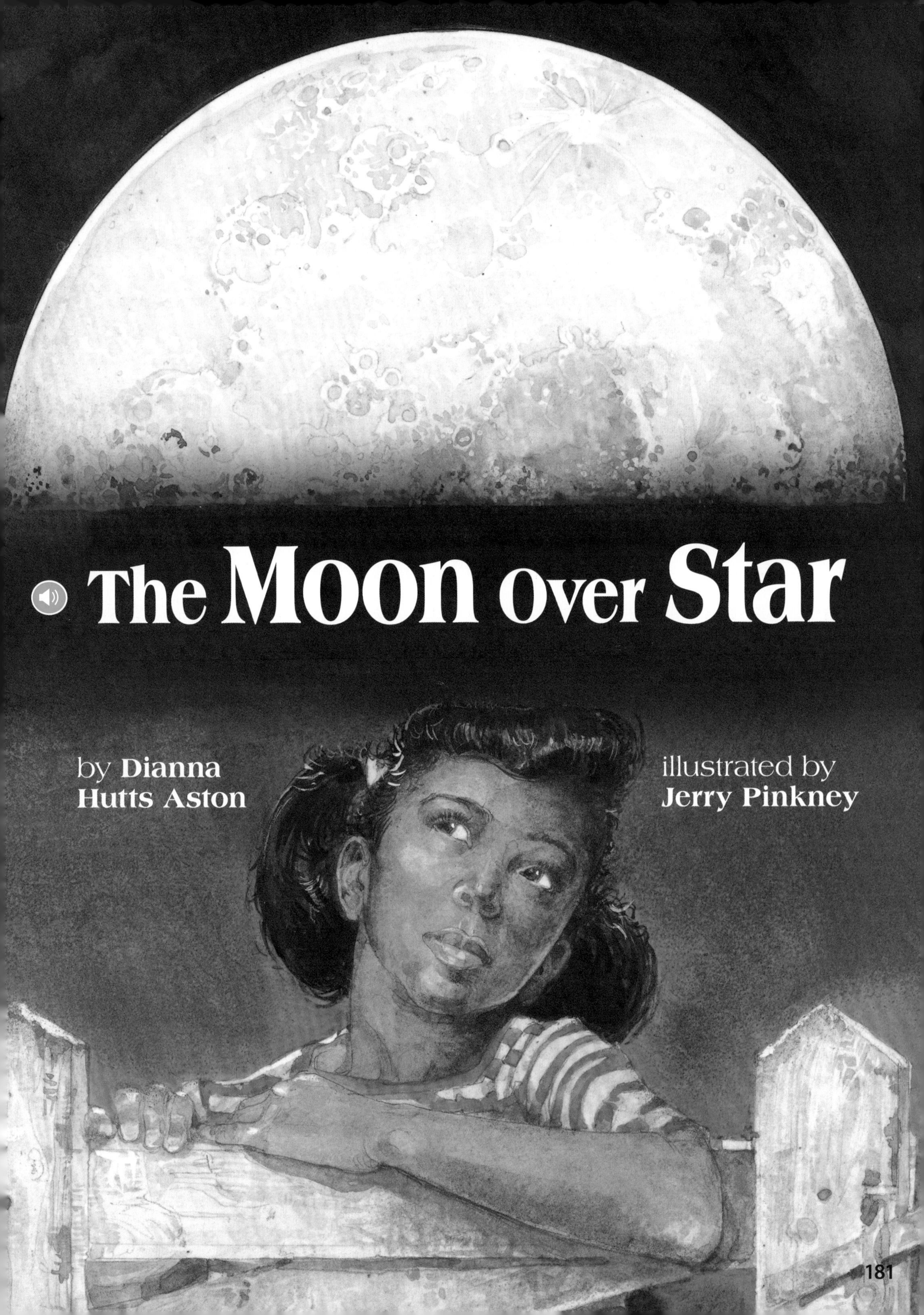

The Moon over Star

by Dianna Hutts Aston

illustrated by Jerry Pinkney

▶ **Set a Purpose**
Find out what one family in the
town of Star thinks of space travel.

It was a summer's morning in 1969, in the town of Star, where I lived. If all went well, a spaceship carrying **astronauts** Neil Armstrong, Edwin Aldrin, Jr., and Michael Collins would land on the moon today. I dreamed that maybe one day, I could go to the moon, too.

My **gramps** thought the space program was a **waste** of money, but I knew he still thought about the astronauts. I thought about the astronauts' kids and wondered if they were scared—scared but proud. I knew I'd be.

gramps grandfather
waste bad use

Once upon a summer's noon, my cousins and I
scouted **Gran's** watermelon patch for the biggest one.
It took three of us to carry it to a tub of ice—three and
a half, counting my littlest cousin, Lacey.

We decorated the picnic table with pails of
wildflowers. Then, our **chores** done, we built our own
spaceship from **scraps** we found in the barn.

Gran's Grandmother's
chores work
scraps pieces or parts of things

As the oldest grandchild, I got to be **launch controller** and Commander Armstrong.

"**Ignition sequence start** . . . 6, 5, 4, 3, 2, 1, 0. Liftoff, we have liftoff!"

We closed our eyes, imagining **with all our might** the rumble, the roar, and the force of the Saturn rocket, blasting the spaceship into the stars. Then we were rushing through space at 25,000 miles per hour.

launch controller the person in charge of the launch

Ignition sequence start Start counting backward

with all our might as hard as we could

"I wonder how many miles it is to the moon," Cousin Carrie said.

I'd been reading the moon stories in the paper, so I knew. "About 240,000 miles," I said. "And some scientists say it's moving away from us—an inch or so farther every year."

I also knew that in May 1961, a month before I was born, President John F. Kennedy had said America would send men to the moon before **the decade was out**.

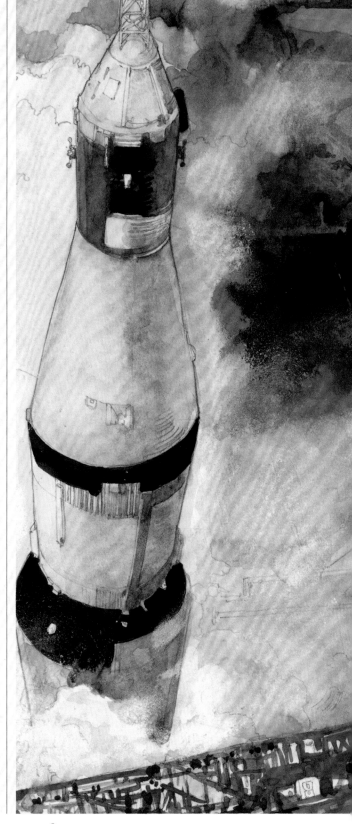

the decade was out the year 1970

▶ **Before You Continue**

1. **Generalize** What is one thing the narrator thinks about space travel?

2. **Make Comparisons** How is the children's game like a real liftoff?

▶ **Predict**
How will Gramps respond when the
first spacecraft lands on the moon?

That afternoon, we were helping
Gramps with the tractor when Gran **hollered**,
"Come quick! They're landing!"

Gramps kept right on **tinkering with** the engine.
The rest of us ran **pell-mell** for the house and squirmed
around the television screen as it glowed with equal
parts of moon and the spaceship called *Eagle*.

We heard the voice of Commander Armstrong
directing the landing. "Forward . . . forward," he said.

hollered yelled
tinkering with working on
pell-mell in a wild rush

Then the newsman we all knew, Walter Cronkite, exclaimed, "Man on the moon!"

For a **split second** we were silent. The whole universe must have been, as we waited to hear the voice of an **astronaut** 240,000 miles away.

And then: **"Houston, Tranquility Base here,"** Commander Armstrong said. **"The *Eagle* has landed."**

split second brief moment

"Tranquility Base here" "I'm calling from Tranquility Base"

"The *Eagle* has landed." "The spacecraft has landed on the moon." ▶

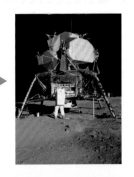

Boy, did we cheer, all of the cousins and even
the grown-ups—all except Gramps. I remembered
something he'd once said:

"Why spend all that money to go to the moon when
there are so many folks **in need** right here on Earth?"

"Because we can!" I'd almost shouted, but **caught**
myself.

I began to wonder then what Gramps's dreams had
been. From the time he was little, he had worked the
farm, doing the same jobs, **day to day**, season to season.

in need who need money
caught stopped
day to day one day after another

When the **crickets began to sing**, Gramps sat down to rest. I pulled off his **dirt-caked** boots for him and stomped around the porch.

"Gramps, will you watch the moon walk with me tonight?"

"I'm **mighty worn out** today," he said, "but maybe."

Suddenly, I could see how tired he was. Lifetime-tired. There were deep lines in his face—a farmer's face, an old farmer's face.

"All right, Gramps," I said. "It's okay."

crickets began to sing evening came
dirt-caked covered in dirt
mighty worn out very tired

▶ Before You Continue

1. **Explain** Why isn't Gramps as excited as everyone else about the moon landing?
2. **Plot** What two events are happening in the story at this point?

▶ **Predict**
What will the moon walk mean to
the narrator?

Once upon a summer's night in 1969,
we spread blankets and folding chairs on the edge of the
yard, where the buffalo grass grew thick and soft. The
cornstalks whispered while we **gazed** at the pearly slice
of moon and the stars, which gleamed like spilled sugar.

What were the **astronauts** seeing, right at this very
second? Could they see beyond the moon, to Mars or
Neptune or Jupiter?

What I could see above me, and what I could see in
my imagination, were better than any **picture** show.

gazed looked
picture movie or television

Later on that summer's night, in 1969, the television screen flashed with words that **gave me goose bumps: LIVE FROM** THE SURFACE OF THE MOON.

Mr. Cronkite said, ". . . Neil Armstrong, thirty-eight-year-old American, standing on the surface of the moon on this July twentieth, nineteen hundred and sixty-nine!"

gave me goose bumps thrilled me
LIVE FROM THIS IS HAPPENING RIGHT NOW ON

I didn't know it then, but there were 600 million people **the world over** watching with me and listening, when Commander Armstrong said, "That's one small step for man, one giant leap for mankind."

All of us—from New York to Tokyo to Paris to Cairo . . . to Star—watched it together, the **astronauts** bounding across the moon like ghosts on a **trampoline**. I felt a hand on my shoulder.

"I **reckon** that's something to remember," Gramps said quietly.

trampoline

the world over all over the world
◄ **trampoline** springy surface
reckon guess

Later, when it was as quiet as the world ever gets, Gramps and I stood together under the moon.

"What's mankind?" I asked him.

"It's all of us," he finally said. "It's all of us who've ever lived, all of us still to come."

I put my hand in his. "Just think, Gramps, if they could go to the moon, maybe one day I could too!"

"Great days," he said, "an **astronaut** in the family. **Who'd a** thought?"

I smiled in the dark. My gramps was proud of me.

Who'd a Who would have

"The first airplane I ever saw, I was your age. It was right over **yonder**," Gramps said, nodding toward the cornfield. "That was something to see."

A sigh in Gramps's voice made my heart squeeze.

"Keep on dreaming, Mae," he said. "Just remember, we're here now together on the prettiest star in **the heavens**."

Gramps had **looked to** the moon all of his life. It told him when to plant and when to harvest. And once upon a summer's night, it told me to dream. ❖

yonder there
the heavens space
looked to depended on

▶ **Before You Continue**
1. **Visualize** What does Mae see when she looks up to the sky? What does she imagine that the **astronauts** see?
2. **Character** How does Gramps change?

Meet the Illustrator

Jerry Pinkney

As a teenager, Jerry Pinkney worked at a newsstand. Every day he drew pictures of the people walking by. One day, a famous cartoonist stopped and gave him advice. That's when Mr. Pinkney realized he could become a professional artist.

Now when Mr. Pinkney starts drawing, he doesn't know exactly what will happen until his pencil touches the paper. "Then the image comes to life", he says. "When I put a line down, the only thing I know is how it should feel."

▲ Jerry Pinkney

Drawing Tip

An illustrator has to use the writer's words to help him picture the characters. How do words like "lifetime-tired" help the artist to draw Gramps?

Think and Respond

Key Words	
astronaut	orbit
capacity	planet
constant	resistance
launch	rotation
limit	technology

Talk About It

1. What seems **realistic** about the story? Give three examples.

   The story is realistic because _____ .

2. Summarize one theme of the story. Explain why you think this is the author's main message. **Clarify** your ideas.

3. Does this story have a first-person narrator or a third-person narrator? Explain how you can tell.

   The story has a _____ . I can tell because _____ .

Write About It

What image does the author use to describe the **astronauts** as they walk on the moon? How does this help you picture what Mae sees? Write a short paragraph. Use **Key Words** to explain your thinking.

The astronauts look like _____ .

Plot

Make a plot diagram to retell the story of "The Moon Over Star." Include the problem, the important events, the turning point, and the solution.

Plot Diagram

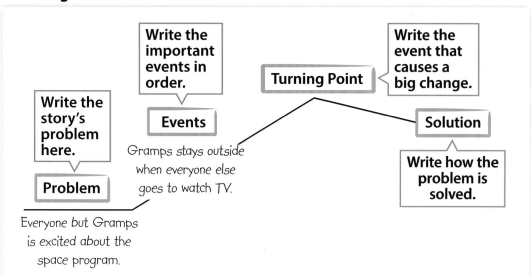

Now use your plot diagram as you retell the story to a partner. Use **Key Words** as you tell what the turning point is and how the problem is solved.

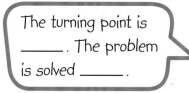

The turning point is _____. The problem is solved _____.

Fluency

Practice reading with expression. Rate your reading.

Role-play a conversation between Mae and Gramps. What does it take to explore space? Use **Key Words** as you answer this question: Is it worth it to explore space?

Word Parts

Many English words are made up of word parts. A **root** is a word part that has meaning. Unlike a base word, though, it cannot stand on its own.

If you know the meaning of a root, you can sometimes figure out the meaning of the whole word.

Astronaut is formed from two roots: **astro** + **naut**. An astronaut is a "star sailor."

Root	Origin	Meaning	Example
astro	Greek	star	astronomy
naut	Greek	sailor	nautical
wis	Old English	wise	wisdom
rota	Latin	wheel	rotation

Try It Together

Answer each question. Use the chart above to help you.

1. What do you think wisdom means?

   A a faraway star

   B someone who lives on a ship

   C a good student

   D good sense

2. What do you think rotary means?

   A a large ship

   B something that turns like a wheel

   C something that is rotten

   D a car

The First Person on the Moon

adapted from the National Aeronautics and Space Administration (NASA) website

On July 20, 1969, **astronaut** Neil Armstrong became the first person to **set foot** on the moon. As the world watched on television, Armstrong stepped onto the moon's surface and spoke these famous words: "One small step for a man, one giant leap for **mankind**."

The astronauts placed an American flag on the moon's surface.

set foot step
mankind people everywhere

▶ **Before You Continue**

1. **Explain** Why was July 20, 1969, an important day in human history?
2. **Paraphrase** What does Armstrong's famous quote mean? Restate it.

The Right Pilot for the Job

This amazing day was the result of years of hard work. In 1961, President John F. Kennedy wanted America to be the first nation to land humans on the moon and bring them back safely. NASA space scientists worked toward that goal for years. At last they were ready to put people on the moon. Neil Armstrong was the perfect person to command the **mission**.

Armstrong was born in 1930 in Wapakoneta, Ohio. He loved flying, and he got his pilot's license at age sixteen. After graduating from college, he became a military pilot. In 1962, Armstrong joined NASA's **astronaut** program.

▲ Neil Armstrong

◀ The **astronauts** left a small golden olive branch on the moon as a symbol of peace.

mission project

In 1969, Armstrong became the commander of Apollo 11, the first **lunar** landing mission. He and his crew, Edwin "Buzz" Aldrin and Michael Collins, fulfilled the dream of a nation. When Apollo 11 returned safely to Earth, Armstrong was greeted as a hero.

Armstrong has received many awards, including the Presidential Medal of Freedom. Although he never walked on the moon again, he helped plan other space missions. He also taught spacecraft design at the University of Cincinnati. But he will always be remembered as the first person on the moon. ❖

lunar moon

Earth

Moon

▲ The **astronauts** begin their return to Earth.

▲ The astronauts were greeted as heroes after the success of Apollo 11.

▶ **Before You Continue**

1. **Generalize** What does it mean to be a hero? How did the **astronauts** fit that meaning?

2. **Goal/Outcome** Compare President Kennedy's goal with the outcome of the Apollo 11 mission.

Respond and Extend

Key Words	
astronaut	orbit
capacity	planet
constant	resistance
launch	rotation
limit	technology

Compare Fiction and Biography

A story that is fiction is not true, even if it includes events that really happened. A biography is nonfiction. It tells a true story.

Compare the story and the biography. What events and facts do both of them tell about? Work with a partner to complete a comparison chart.

Comparison Chart

Put a checkmark if it gives the fact.

Event or Fact	"The Moon Over Star"	"The First Person on the Moon"
Neil Armstrong was born in 1930.		✓
In 1961, President Kennedy said that America would send people to the moon.	✓	✓
Armstrong, Aldrin, and Collins flew to the moon in the summer of 1969.		
Armstrong was the commander of the mission.		
The first person to walk on the moon was Armstrong.		
The world watched on television.		
Armstrong said, "One small step for man, one giant leap for mankind."		
The astronauts placed a flag on the moon.		
The moon is 240,000 miles from Earth.		

Talk Together

What did it take for the **astronauts** to explore the moon? Think about the story and the biography. Use **Key Words** to to talk about your ideas.

Prepositional Phrases

A **prepositional phrase** starts with a **preposition** and ends with a noun or a pronoun. Use prepositional phrases in these ways:

Grammar Rules Prepositional Phrases	
• to show where something is	Earth orbits the sun **between** **Venus and Mars**.
• to show time	**After** sunset, the moon rose.
• to show direction	A meteor flew **across** the sky.
• to add details	The space ship landed **with** a thud. The astronauts worked **as** a team.

Read Prepositional Phrases

Read this passage from "Moon Over Star." Can you find four prepositional phrases? They start with the prepositions *with, of, into,* and *through.*

> We closed our eyes, imagining with all our might the rumble, the roar, and the force of the Saturn rocket, blasting the spaceship into the stars. Then we were rushing through space at 25,000 miles per hour.

Write Prepositional Phrases

Write a short paragraph about exploring space. Use at least three prepositional phrases to describe the event.

Write About Yourself
Write a Personal Narrative

Tell about an experience that changed the way you thought about "fast." You and your classmates will collect your stories in a book called, *How Fast Is Fast?*

Study a Model

A personal narrative is a true story about something important. Read Stacey's story about her sister's race.

The first lines capture the reader's interest.

The middle gives details to help readers understand the experience.

My Sister, the Turtle

by Stacey Allen

My sister, Alyssa, should never have been a runner. She's got such short legs! But she always loved to run.

In middle school, **Alyssa joined the track team**. She was so slow, even her friends called her "Turtle."

"Why don't you quit?" I asked.

"Because I'm going to get better," she told me. At her first track meet, Alyssa was going to run the 100-meter dash. I almost stayed home. I didn't want to see her lose.

The race began. Alyssa was the last one off the starting blocks. But then she started to pass the other runners.

The Turtle came in third. As for me, **I learned that you should never give up doing what you love.**

The beginning tells what the experience is all about.

The ending tells why the experience was important.

Prewrite

1. **Choose a Topic** What experience will you write about? Talk with a partner to choose one.

Language Frames	
Tell Your Ideas	**Respond to Ideas**
• One of my favorite memories is _____ . • I once knew someone who _____ . • I never knew what _____ meant until _____ .	• Tell me why _____ was important to you. • _____ sounds interesting. I'd like to read about it because _____ . • I'm not sure _____ would make a good story. Tell me more.

2. **Gather Information** Recall the details about where and when your event took place. Tell who was involved. Write down how you felt about what happened.

3. **Get Organized** Use a chart or map to help you organize your details. Stacey used a comparison chart to show how her feelings changed.

Comparison Chart

Before the Race	During the Race	After the Race
I thought Alyssa wasn't a good runner.	I didn't want to go to the race.	Alyssa was fast!

Draft

Use your chart and details to write your draft. Tell what happened and how the experience affected you. Try to use dialogue to make the story more interesting.

Revise

1. **Read, Retell, Respond** Read your draft aloud to a partner. Your partner listens and then retells the story. Then talk about ways to improve your writing.

Language Frames	
Retell	**Make Suggestions**
• You told about a time when _____ .	• I can't really picture _____ .
• At first, you felt _____ . Later, you felt _____ .	• Maybe you could say more about how you felt about _____ .
• The experience was important to you because _____ .	• Some of the sentences don't sound like you. One example is _____ .

2. **Make Changes** Think about your draft and your partner's suggestions. Then use revision marks to make your changes.

   • Could dialogue make your story more interesting? See if there are places you could add some.

   > "Why don't you quit?" I asked.
   > ⋀Could you please answer some questions?

   • Does your writing sound like you? Make sure you've used your own voice.

   > She was so slow, even her friends called her "Turtle."
   > Alyssa joined the track team. ⋀She wasn't a fast runner.

Edit and Proofread

Work with a partner to edit and proofread your personal narrative. Be sure your sentences have meaningful details. Use revision marks to show your changes.

Grammar Tip

Use prepositional phrases to add details. Some common prepositions are *above, between, during,* and *through.*

Present

On Your Own Make a final copy of your personal narrative. Choose a way to share it with your classmates. You can read it aloud or you can have someone record you telling it.

Presentation Tips	
If you are the speaker...	**If you are the listener...**
Use gestures to emphasize important parts of your story.	Think about why the writer chose to tell about this event.
If you are retelling your personal narrative, be sure to present events in the right order.	Decide what message the writer is trying to share through this narrative.

In a Group Collect all of the personal narratives from your class. Bind them into a book called *How Fast Is Fast?* Share the book with friends. You could also choose to record your narratives. If you do, include photographs from the real events.

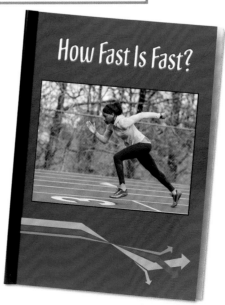

How Fast Is Fast?

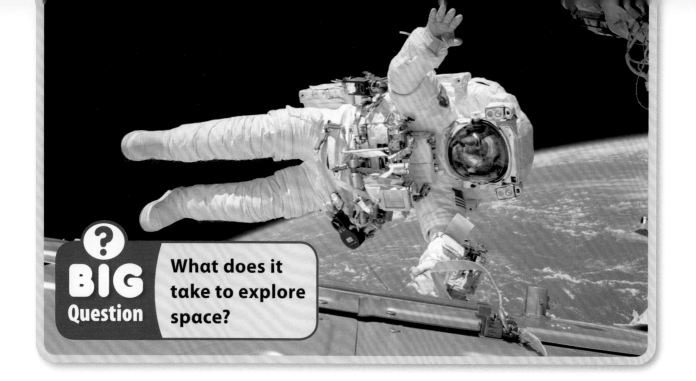

What does it take to explore space?

In this unit, you found lots of answers to the **Big Question**. Now, make a concept map to discuss the **Big Question** with the class.

Concept Map

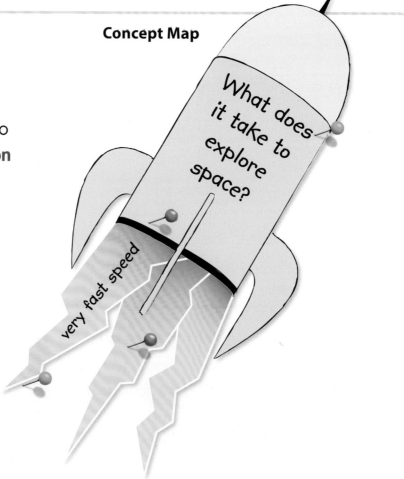

What does it take to explore space?

very fast speed

Write a Note

Use your concept map. Write a note to a friend explaining whether or not you would like to explore space. Explain your answer.

Share Your Ideas

Choose one of these ways to share your ideas about the **Big Question**.

Write It!

Write a Story

Write a story about a fast-moving creature. How would the creature use speed to do things? Make the plot exciting! Include details about the setting and characters. Illustrate your story.

Talk About It!

Give an Interview

Imagine you were the first person on the moon. Give an interview to tell about your experiences. Tell how you felt, what you saw, and what people should know about the moon.

Do It!

Model the Earth, Sun, and Moon

With a small group, show how Earth moves around the sun. Then show how the moon revolves around Earth. Give clear, step-by-step instructions so your classmates can follow.

Earth

Sun

Write It!

Make a Packing List

Imagine that the space program asked you to travel to the moon for one week. What would you bring? Make a packing list. Include personal things and tools for your moon study.

Unit 8

Saving a Piece of the World

BIG Question

? What's worth protecting?

BANNOCKBURN, SCOTLAND
A worker starting restoration work on a historical statue

Share What You Know

Do It!

① **Think** of a brave character from a movie or TV show.

② **Pantomime** a scene that shows how the character might act to help someone in need.

③ **Take** a vote. Which character does your class think is bravest? Why?

Heroes

Express Opinions

Listen to Beatriz's song. Then use **Language Frames** to express an opinion about a problem that you can help solve.

Song

One Kid Can

When your town has a problem,

Remember this inspiring song.

I don't believe that it's

    too difficult

To change something

    that's wrong.

One kid can make a difference.

Yes, I do think that

    one kid can.

It only takes one

    good idea

For us to start a

    perfect plan.

Tune: "Give My Regards
   to Broadway"

🔊 Key Words

Look at the pictures. Use **Key Words** and other words as you talk about what makes someone a **hero**.

Who Is a Hero?

A **volunteer** works without pay. These volunteers serve food to people in need.

Park rangers often teach park visitors about animals and how to **protect** them.

Some workers keep a national **heritage** alive. This one teaches about a Native American way of life.

A **president** leads a nation.

Talk Together

What things of value do heroes protect? Try to use Language Frames from page 212 and Key Words to **express opinions** to a partner.

Goal and Outcome

A **goal** is something you want to achieve. The **outcome** is whether or not you actually reach your goal.

Look at the pictures of Beatriz's project. Keep track of goals and outcomes to understand how and why things happen.

Map and Talk

You can make a goal-and-outcome map to track someone's progress. Write the goal on the first step. Use the next steps to list events that happen on the way to reaching the goal. Write the outcome on the last step.

Goal-and-Outcome Map

Beatriz wants to make her street greener.
Goal

She calls the Green Team.
Event 1

They plant young trees.
Event 2

The trees grow. The street gets very green!
Outcome

Talk **Together**

Tell a partner about a project you completed. Use a goal-and-outcome map to describe your goal and the steps you followed to reach it.

◑ More Key Words

Use these words to talk about "Buffalo Music" and "Saving Bison from Extinction."

mission
noun

A **mission** is a job with a goal. Their **mission** is to rescue people after an earthquake.

motive
noun

A **motive** is a reason for doing something. One **motive** for studying is to get good grades.

responsible
adjective

A person who is **responsible** is in charge. This dad is **responsible** for his son.

service
noun

When something is of **service**, it is useful. A cart is of **service** when you move heavy boxes.

value
verb

To **value** something is to care about it. Many people **value** saving money.

Talk Together

Talk with a partner. Tell how each **Key Word** makes you feel. Say why.

> _Value_ reminds me that I believe my family is valuable. It makes me feel good!

Choose Reading Strategies

As you read, you use different strategies to help you understand a text's meaning. Often, you use more than one strategy. You just need to know which strategies to use and when to use them. As you read:

- Think about the different strategies you have in your mental toolbox.

- Know what you are reading. Some strategies are better than others for each type of text.

- Be flexible. Sometimes you need to stop using one strategy and try another. Even the best readers switch and add strategies!

When you read, choose a reading strategy to help you understand.

Reading Strategies
• Preview and Predict
• Monitor and Clarify
• Make Connections
• Visualize
• Ask Questions
• Make Inferences
• Identify Main Idea and Details
• Summarize
• Draw Conclusions
• Form Generalizations

How to Choose a Reading Strategy

1. Think about what you are trying to understand.

   I don't understand _____ .

2. Decide which strategy you can use to help you understand the text.

   I can _____ .

3. Think about how the strategy helped you.

   That strategy helped me _____ .

Read Beatriz's poem. Practice the reading strategies. Tell a partner which strategies you used to help you understand the poem.

Poem

A Million Trees

Let's get down on our knees
and plant a million trees!
My **mission** sounds unlikely,
but I think we can do it.
We only have one planet.
Planting trees will help renew it.
Our **motive** is simple—
We want to see more green.
We'll plant from Maine to Oregon
and everywhere between.
Let's all be **responsible**.
We'll make the planet greener.
The trees will be of **service**.
The air will be much cleaner.
Let's show we **value** nature
by helping to restore it.
Let's plant a million trees—
The squirrels will adore it!

Read a Story

Genre

Historical fiction is a story that takes place in the past. It is based on real events. The writer adds events that could have happened.

Setting

The setting of a story is where and when the events happen. In historical fiction, the setting is usually tied to the events in the story.

▲ The setting of this story is Palo Duro Canyon in northern Texas, in the late 1800s.

Buffalo Music

by Tracey E. Fern ♦ illustrated by Greg Shed

▶ **Set a Purpose**
Find out what "buffalo music"
means to the narrator of this story.

When I first settled here on Palo Duro Canyon, I had no company except for the animals. I woke to the **reveille** of the roosters. I did chores to the **choir** of the crows. I dreamed to the **chorus** of the coyotes. Mostly, though, I lived to the music of the buffalo.

I stirred the fire to the *huff-huff* of buffalo breath clouding the chill dawn. I gardened to the *scritch-scritch* of buffalo scratching themselves against the cottonwoods.

I swept the **dugout** to the thunder of buffalo as they drifted like a dark cloud across the prairie. That buffalo music played right to my heart.

reveille morning song
choir singing
chorus howls; cries
◀ **dugout** house that is
dug in the ground

One day, different sounds filled the canyon. They were the boom and blast of rifles.

"What are those shots?" I asked my husband, Charlie.

"Buffalo hunters, Molly," he said. "They're trying to **turn a profit** on **hides** and hooves."

It seemed as if every man in Texas was **afire to make a fortune** in the buffalo business. Day after day, the hunters galloped into the heart of the **herd**. Shots echoed over the hills and through the hollows from sunup till sundown. And day after day, another hundred or more buffalo lay dead.

turn a profit make money
hides buffalo skins
afire to make a fortune wanting to get rich
herd group of buffalo

That summer, the heat fell as heavy as an angry fist. The trails were **deep** with dust. The grass cracked like glass **underfoot**. And everywhere, as far as the eye could see, the bleached bones of the buffalo **glistened** white in the sun.

Within six seasons, the hunters were gone. So was the buffalo music.

Oh, those were lonely, silent days! I was sure the only song left in the canyon was the cold whistle of the north wind.

deep filled
underfoot as we stepped on it
glistened shined

But one spring morning, I was **lugging** wash water up from the river when a cowhand named Billie came trotting up.

"Howdy, Miss Molly," Billie said. "I've got some **orphans** for you."

Billie knew I had **a soft spot for critters**. He'd bring me whatever stray or sickly creature he found on the trail—prairie dogs, wolf pups, wild turkeys. Once, he even brought me an antelope.

"What did you bring this time?" I asked Billie as I set down the water and went to have a look.

Two buffalo calves were trailing after him, as skinny as hungry snakes.

lugging carrying

orphans young creatures that don't
    have parents

a soft spot for critters always liked
    animals

▶ **Before You Continue**

1. **Theme** What does "buffalo music" mean to Molly?

2. **Figurative Language** What would grass that "cracked like glass underfoot" look and feel like?

223

▶ **Predict**
What will Molly do with
the buffalo calves?

"**I** found them **snoozing** under a **juniper**," Billie said. "Hunters must have figured they were too **puny to fuss with**. Do you think you can fatten them up?"

Right then, one of the calves let out a soft snort. That sound brought back some memories. I didn't need to hear anything else before making up my mind.

"I **can't tell** till I try," I told Billie. "Let's get them inside before the wolves find them."

snoozing sleeping
◀ **juniper** small tree with berrylike cones
puny to fuss with small to hunt
can't tell won't know

I know that some people think I'm as tough as old **beef jerky**. The truth is, I'd seen too many living things **disappear** in the hard struggle for life here. I **wasn't about** to let the buffalo go, too.

Those calves followed me back to the dugout, **strolled** in through the front door, and lay down in front of the fire. I named one Calico, because she was the same faded red as my favorite dress. I called the other one Chester, after a neighbor back home in Tennessee with the same fierce-eyed stare.

calico ▶

beef jerky dried meat
disappear die
wasn't about didn't want
strolled walked slowly

Then I got to work caring for them. I **tucked** hot-water bottles inside flannel cloth and wrapped a cloth around each calf. I fed them like babies, squeezing cow's milk from a rag.

Those calves sure could drink—three gallons a day or more! Feeding them kept me so busy that I hardly had time to blink.

Charlie just shook his head at me. "**Tending to** those two **runts** won't change anything," he told me.

But Charlie knew better than to waste his breath arguing with me. I was determined to hear buffalo music again in this lifetime.

tucked put
Tending to Taking care of
runts small, weak animals

Within a few weeks, Calico and Chester were as **plump** as biscuit dumplings! By then, Charlie was tired of having wild critters in the dugout. He fenced off a section of pasture, and I turned the calves loose with the milking cows.

Pretty soon, word **got out** all over **the Panhandle** that I was tending buffalo calves. Every time a cowhand rode up with another orphan, Charlie would sigh and start **stoking** the dugout fire.

plump fat
got out spread
the Panhandle this part of Texas
stoking stirring

▶ **Before You Continue**

1. **Goal/Outcome** What is Molly's goal? How does she try to achieve it?
2. **Make Connections** How would you feel if you were Charlie?

▶ **Predict**
Will Molly achieve her goal?

Maybe Charlie was right. The wild herds probably were long gone, like dew before the sun. But I knew there was another way to end the silence in the canyon. I could start a herd of my own.

I got to work feeding and watering my orphans, **mending** the sick, and **fending off** wolves and **poachers** with the long end of my rifle. With time and tending, my little herd grew. Soon I had one hundred **head**.

mending healing
fending off scaring away
poachers hunters
head buffalo

Then one day, word came that Yellowstone National Park wanted to rebuild its buffalo herd. As soon as I heard that, I got to work.

I drove Calico and Chester and two **yearlings** to the east edge of our **spread**, where the Santa Fe railway line came through. I set Billie to work building four **timber stalls spiked to** the frame of a **boxcar**. We fastened some thick padding to keep the buffalo safe from the swaying and jostling of the train. Then I loaded up the boxcar with bales of hay and barrels of water.

yearlings one-year-old buffalo
spread land
timber stalls spiked to wood containers
    attached to
boxcar railroad car

I couldn't leave the rest of my herd. Billie would tend these four till they got settled on their new **range**. "Take good care of them," I told Billie as he climbed aboard the train.

I stood watching, till the last hollow echo of the train whistle faded. "Good luck to you, my old friends," I whispered.

When Billie wrote a few months later, he had some big news. Calico had given birth to a healthy calf. That was some day! **To my way of thinking**, it wasn't just the birth of a calf. It was the **rebirth** of our national herd.

range land; home
To my way of thinking
 In my opinion
rebirth revival

The sounds of the canyon are different now.
Settlers have crowded in. Fences and longhorns
dot the land as far as the eye can see. Nowadays,
I wake to the rumble of engines, do chores to the
whoop and holler of a hundred cowhands, and go
to sleep to the blast of the train whistles.

longhorn

dot cover
whoop and holler shouting

But some days when I ride north beyond the last **stand of salt cedar**, I can once again hear the faint chords of the old songs. I hear the clatter of clashing horns. I hear the bellowing of the bulls. I hear the muffled thud of hooves as they hurl up dust. And I live **on the keen edge of** hope that one day the **strains** of that sweet, wild music will echo far beyond these canyon walls. ❖

stand of salt cedar group of trees
on the keen edge of with the
strains sounds

▶ **Before You Continue**

1. **Goal/Outcome** Does Molly achieve her goal? Explain.
2. **Visualize** What do you think Molly is picturing when she describes the sounds she hopes to hear again?

Meet the Author

Tracey E. Fern

Like Molly, Tracey E. Fern loves the sights and sounds of nature. When she was young, she lived near a beach. She says, "If I walked far enough along that beach, there were no houses and no people— just water and birds and sand and sky. It was the perfect place to dream."

As a child, Tracey E. Fern dreamed of writing books. When she grew up, she did it! Many of her books and stories are historical fiction.

Tracey E. Fern still loves walking along the beach and dreaming. Now she dreams about the books she plans to write.

Tracey E. Fern ▶

Writing Tip ✏️

Tracey E. Fern writes: "...the heat fell as heavy as an angry fist." Find other examples of figurative language in "Buffalo Music." Then use figurative language to write your own description of something in nature.

Think and Respond

Key Words

heritage	protect
hero	responsible
mission	service
motive	value
president	volunteer

Talk About It

1. What clues tell you that this story is **historical fiction**?

   _____ really happened, but _____ is/are made up.

2. Do you think the main character of this story is a **hero**? **Express** your **opinion** to a partner. Use the text to support your opinion. Speak clearly and check that your partner understands you.

3. How does the story's main message, or theme, relate to **protecting** things that are endangered? Give a brief summary of the story to a partner. Then explain how the story events relate to the theme.

Write About It

This story includes many details about nature. Think of something in nature that you think is worth protecting. Write a short rhyming poem to describe it. Use sensory details and **Key Words**, if possible.

I'd like to save a _____.

Goal and Outcome

Make a goal-and-outcome map for "Buffalo Music." Notice how each event leads to the next.

Goal-and-Outcome Map

Goal

Write Molly's goal here.

Event 1

Write each event that helps her reach her goal. You can add more events.

Event 2

Billie brings her two buffalo calves.

Event 3

Outcome

Write the outcome here.

Now use your goal-and-outcome map as you retell the story to a partner. Use **Key Words**.

Molly wants to _____ .
First, _____ . . . .
The outcome is _____ .

Fluency

Practice reading with intonation. Rate your reading.

Talk Together

What does Molly think is worth **protecting**, and why? Do you agree? Why or why not? Use **Key Words** as you discuss your ideas.

More Idioms

An **idiom** is a colorful way to say something. Sometimes you can use context clues to figure out what an idiom means.

What you say:	What you mean:
The mayor **sings Bill's praises**. 	The mayor **thinks Bill deserves recognition**. 

Try It Together

Read the paragraph. Use context clues to figure out the meaning. Then answer the questions.

My hero is my Uncle Dave. He is a veterinarian, which means he cares for animals. He is <u>as sharp as a tack</u>! He can spot a sick animal <u>in the blink of an eye</u>, and he always knows how to help.

1. **As sharp as a tack most likely means**

   A not very smart.

   B very smart.

   C has pointy fingers.

   D is always sad.

2. **In the blink of an eye probably means**

   A with his eyes open.

   B with his back turned.

   C all day long.

   D very quickly.

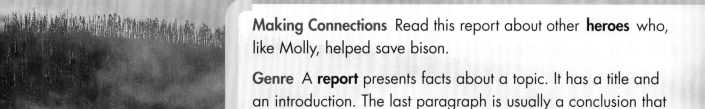

SAVING Bison FROM Extinction

by **Dorothy Young**

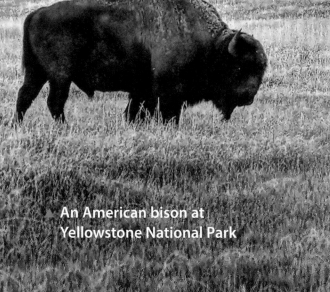

An American bison at Yellowstone National Park

At one time, 25 to 50 million American bison, often called buffalo, lived in North America. Many Native American groups depended on the animals for food, clothing, and shelter. They used almost every part of the animal.

Extinction Dying Out As a Species

▸ **Before You Continue**

1. **Use Text Features** Read the title and look at the photo on this page. Together, what do they tell you about the topic?

2. **Visualize** What do you think clothing made from buffalo feels like? Why?

The Importance of Bison to Native Americans

Bison had always been important to Native Americans of the **Plains**. For hundreds of years, many Native Americans depended on bison for survival. Bison were part of their culture.

Many Native Americans used bison meat for food. They used their hides for gloves, **moccasins**, and **tepee** coverings. They even used the bones for tools and decorations.

▲ **Bison provided food, clothing, and shelter for Native Americans of the Plains.**

Plains flat lands
◀ **moccasins** shoes
tepee tent

Bison in Danger

European settlers also hunted bison, but not just for food. They wanted to remove bison from the land so they could start farms. They also hunted bison for **sport and profit**. As settlers moved west, they killed more and more bison.

Railroads and Bison

Railroads helped settle the West. But they were not good for the bison. Hunters shot bison to feed the workers who were laying railroad tracks.

Sometimes train operators slowed their engines when they spotted bison. They let passengers shoot the animals from train windows.

Railroads allowed hunters to send bison hides to the cities. People in cities made leather from bison hides.

By 1890 only about 1,000 bison remained.

▲ Bison hunters in 1882

▲ Workers lay new track for the railroad.

sport and profit fun and to make money

▶ **Before You Continue**

1. **Generalize** How did some Native Americans of the Plains depend on bison?
2. **Summarize** How did railroads affect bison? What do you think "Railroads helped settle the West" means?

Settlers Follow the Railroad

Railroads united the country. They joined the East Coast to the West Coast. Trains also made it easier for people to travel great distances across the Plains. Many settlers traveled to the West by train. As more people traveled to the West, the number of bison decreased.

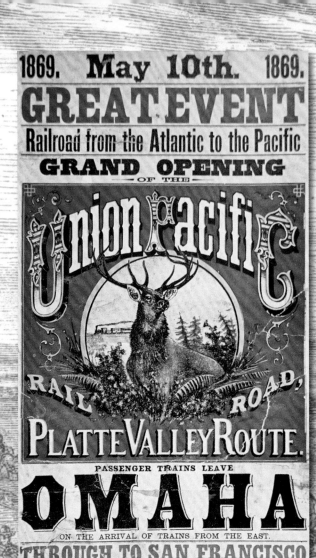

1869. **May 10th.** 1869.
GREAT EVENT
Railroad from the Atlantic to the Pacific
GRAND OPENING
— OF THE —
Union Pacific
RAIL ROAD,
PLATTE VALLEY ROUTE.

PASSENGER TRAINS LEAVE
OMAHA
ON THE ARRIVAL OF TRAINS FROM THE EAST.
THROUGH TO SAN FRANCISCO
In less than Four Days, avoiding the Dangers of the Sea!

Travelers for Pleasure, Health or Business
Will find a Trip over The Rocky Mountains Healthy and Pleasant.

LUXURIOUS CARS & EATING HOUSES
ON THE UNION PACIFIC RAIL ROAD.

PULLMAN'S PALACE SLEEPING CARS
RUN WITH ALL THROUGH PASSENGER TRAINS.

GOLD, SILVER AND OTHER MINERS!
Now is the time to seek your Fortunes in Nebraska, Wyoming, Arizona, Washington, Dakotah Colorado, Utah, Oregon, Montana, New Mexico, Idaho, Nevada or California.

CONNECTIONS MADE AT
DENVER CENTRAL CITY & SANTA FE

Rich Farming Lands!
For Sale **VERY CHEAP** by the
Union Pacific Railroad Company.
The Best Investment! No Fluctuations!
Always Improving in Value.
The Wealth of the Country is made by the advance in Real Estate.
NOW IS THE TIME!
MILLIONS OF ACRES
Of the finest lands on the Continent, in Eastern Nebraska, now for sale, **Many of them never before in Market**, at prices that **Defy Competition.**
FIVE AND TEN YEARS' CREDIT GIVEN, WITH INTEREST AT SIX PER CENT.
The Land Grant Bonds of the Company taken at p for lands. ☞ Full particulars given, new Guide w new Maps mailed free.
THE PIONEER,
A handsome Illustrated paper, containing the F stead Law, sent free to all parts of the world. A
O. F. DAVIS
Land Commissioner U. P
Omaha,

Ads like these encouraged many settlers to move to the West.

FARMS AND HOMES
IN KANSAS!
EMIGRANTS, LOOK TO YOUR INTERESTS.
FARMS AT $3 PER ACRE,
AND NOT A FOOT OF WASTE LAND!
Farms on Ten Years Credit!
And on Purchase, no portion of the Principal Required.
Lands not Taxable for Six Years!!
FARMING LANDS IN
EASTERN KANSAS,
But one hour's ride from the city of Atchison and the Missouri river, are offered on terms which guarantee to the Actual Settler larger benefits than can be secured under the Homestead Act.
THE CENTRAL BRANCH UNION PACIFIC R. R. CO
Offer for Sale their Lands in the Co
KICKAPOO

▲ William Hornaday, pictured here with a bison calf, believed nature was worth **protecting**.

▲ In 1899, bison were also kept at the U.S. National Zoo in Washington D.C.

promote support

William Hornaday Takes Action

In 1889, William Hornaday from the New York Zoological Society discovered that bison were in danger of becoming extinct. He decided to do something about the problem. "It is the duty of every good citizen," he said, "to **promote** the protection of forests and wildlife."

In 1899, Hornaday brought a small group of bison to the new Bronx Zoo. He got the bison from private herds, not from the wild. These herds were owned by individual ranchers.

In 1905, Hornaday and others formed the American Bison Society to **protect** the remaining bison from hunters. Hornaday's work helped save the bison from becoming extinct.

▶ **Before You Continue**

1. **Evaluate** How would the ads on page 240 prompt people to move to the West? What were negative effects of ads like this?

2. **Clarify** How did Hornaday demonstrate his idea of being a "good citizen"?

Samuel Walking Coyote Starts a Herd

Samuel Walking Coyote also helped save bison from extinction. Walking Coyote was a Kalispel from the Flathead **Reservation** in Montana. He was hunting buffalo with a group of **Blackfeet** one winter day in 1872. Eight calves wandered into the camp. The calves were orphans.

Walking Coyote took the orphan calves back home and kept them. His small herd grew. Eventually, he sold it. The new owners allowed the herd to roam freely on the Flathead Reservation.

▲ The yellow area shows where bison roamed wild before the 1800s.

Flathead Reservation in 1906 ▶

Starting Supper. Flathead Reservation
Copyright 1908, by N. A. Forsyth, Butte.

Reservation lands set aside for Native Americans

Blackfeet Native Americans from another group

Bison Today

For some Native Americans, bison are a symbol of their culture and strength. Many groups, such as the Blackfeet in Montana, are working to bring more bison back to their natural habitat.

▲ The yellow areas show where American bison roam wild today.

Today, the United States has more than 200,000 bison. Many of these are **offspring** from Walking Coyote's original herd.

There are now bison herds in South Dakota, Texas, and several other states. Thanks to the efforts of a few **determined** people, bison are no longer in danger of extinction. ❖

Yellowstone National Park in Wyoming has the largest population of free-roaming plains bison on public land.

offspring animals born
determined hard-working

▶ **Before You Continue**

1. **Make Comparisons** What do the maps on pages 242–243 show?
2. **Summarize** What is the conclusion of this report? Explain it in your own words.

Respond and Extend

Key Words

heritage	protect
hero	responsible
mission	service
motive	value
president	volunteer

Compare Fiction and Nonfiction

"Buffalo Music" and "Saving Bison from Extinction" have a similar topic. Make a Venn diagram to compare the ideas in the story and the report. Work with a partner.

Venn Diagram

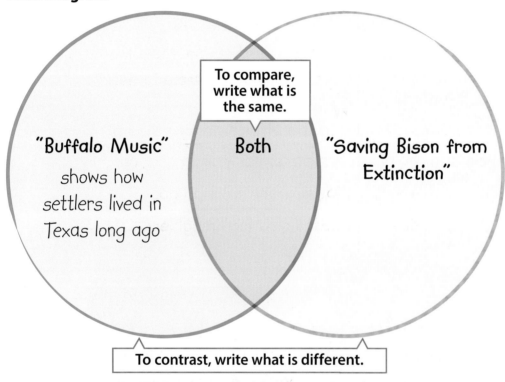

To compare, write what is the same.

"Buffalo Music"
shows how settlers lived in Texas long ago

Both

"Saving Bison from Extinction"

To contrast, write what is different.

Talk Together

What do Molly, Samuel Walking Coyote, and William Hornaday think is worth **protecting**? Why? Think about the story and the report. Use **Key Words** to talk about your ideas.

Past Tense

Regular past-tense verbs end in *-ed*. However, **irregular** past-tense verbs have other forms.

Grammar Rules Past-Tense Verbs

	Now	In the Past
• To form some regular past-tense verbs, you have to change the base word before you add **-ed**.	care	People **cared** about what happened to endangered animals.
	chop	After people **chopped** down the trees, birds had nowhere to nest.
	try	We **tried** to help.
• You just have to remember the forms for irregular past tense verbs.	**go**	The volunteers **went** to help out.
	know	No one **knew** what to do.
	see	Lindsay **saw** the firefighters.

Read Past-Tense Verbs

Read aloud this passage from "Buffalo Music." Find three regular past-tense verbs and two irregular past-tense verbs.

> Those calves followed me back to the dugout, strolled in through the front door, and lay down in front of the fire. I named one Calico, because she was the same faded red as my favorite dress.

Write Past-Tense Verbs

Write a paragraph about a time in the past when you felt like a hero. Use past-tense verbs. Share with a partner.

Justify

Listen to the dialogue between Tierra and Oksana.
Then use **Language Frames** to justify a belief, or to explain why you think your views on an important topic are right. Be sure to support your views and speak clearly.

Dialogue

1

Let's give this to someone in our community. Who do you think should get it?

I think firefighters are the bravest people.

2

Why do you think so?

They save people from danger. And they fight fires that could destroy buildings.

3

That's true. They risk their lives.

That's why I believe firefighters deserve our prize.

🔊 Key Words

Look at the pictures. Use **Key Words** to tell what you know about protecting **ancient** ruins.

Long ago, the Maya culture spread across what is now Mexico and Central America. The Mayans did not create an **empire**, however. Their cities were mostly independent.

Tikal is one of many **sites** from the ancient Maya **civilization**.

Objects such as carvings and drawings provide a **record** of how Mayans lived.

Talk Together

Are ancient ruins worth protecting? Why or why not? Try to use **Language Frames** from page 246 and **Key Words** to **justify** your answer.

Fact and Opinion

A **fact** is something you can check to see if it's true. An **opinion** is what someone thinks or feels.

Look at the poster.

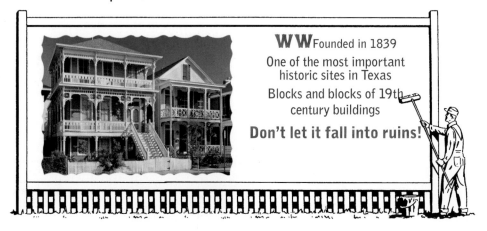

Map and Talk

You can make a fact-and-opinion chart to sort out information you read, see, or hear.

Fact-and-Opinion Chart

Facts	Opinions
Galveston is in Texas.	It's an important historic site.
It was founded in 1839.	The buildings are beautiful.
Historic Galveston covers many blocks.	They need to be taken care of.

List information that you can check as true.

List beliefs or feelings here.

Talk Together

Tell a partner about an advertisement, poster, or flyer. Talk about how the pictures and words tell the message. Use a fact-and-opinion chart to sort the ideas.

🔊 More Key Words

Use these words to talk about "Tutankhamun's Treasures" and "Saving the World's Oldest Library."

courage
noun

If you have **courage**, you are brave. It takes **courage** to do challenging things.

official
adjective

When something is **official**, it's approved. This **official** seal is from the president's office.

principle
noun

A **principle** is a rule or law. Some U.S.A. laws are based on the **principles** of freedom.

project
noun

A **project** is a job or activity. Building a skyscraper is a huge **project**.

risk
noun

Risk is the possibility of harm. Wearing a helmet lowers your **risk** when you ride a bike.

Talk Together

Use a **Key Word** to ask a question. Your partner uses a different **Key Word** to answer.

When do you show <u>courage</u>?

When I take <u>risks</u>.

Reading Strategies

- Preview and Predict
- Monitor and Clarify
- Make Connections
- Visualize
- Ask Questions
- Make Inferences
- Identify Main Idea and Details
- Summarize
- Draw Conclusions
- Form Generalizations

Use Reading Strategies

When do you use reading strategies? You can use reading strategies before, during, and after you read. Here's how to read actively:

- Look through the text to get an idea of what it will be about. Decide on your purpose, or reason for reading.

- While you read, stop now and then to ask yourself: "Does this make sense?" Use a reading strategy to help you better understand the text.

- When you are finished reading, spend some time thinking about the text. Decide what you have learned.

How to Use a Reading Strategy

💭	**1.** Before you begin a text, stop and think: "What strategies can help me get ready to read?"	Before I read, I will _____ .
💭	**2.** While reading, think about what strategies can help you understand.	As I read, I can _____ .
	3. After reading, ask yourself: "What strategies can I use to help me think about what I read?"	Now that I'm done, I think _____ .

Read Tierra's speech. Practice using different reading strategies. Tell a partner which strategies you used and how they helped you understand the speech.

Speech

Protect Our Past!

We should save our petroglyphs now. If we do not protect them, we could lose an important part of our past. We should start a **project** to make sure they are safe.

Petroglyphs are **ancient** rock carvings. These amazing pictures are a **record** of an early **civilization**. Many **sites** with petroglyphs are at **risk**.

Some petroglyphs have been destroyed to build new highways. There should be an **official** rule: Highways should follow other routes.

People can also cause trouble. Some people paint over the carvings, destroying them. Sometimes they just carve other designs nearby. We must have the **courage** to stop this.

We must stand up for our **principles**! Petroglyphs are more than just incredible **objects**. They are our past.

Read a Story

Genre

Historical fiction is a story that takes place in the past. It is based on real events. The writer adds events that could have happened.

Text Feature

Maps can show where important events in the narrative took place.

This story takes place in Egypt and in England.

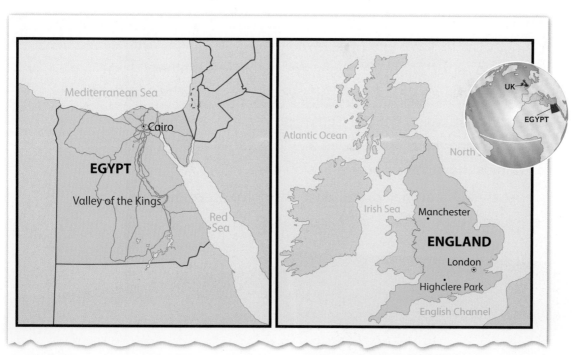

▲ Egypt is a country in Africa and Asia.

▲ The United Kingdom is in Europe. England is one of the four countries in the United Kingdom.

TUTANKHAMUN'S TREASURES

by
Eloise Vivanco

Inspired by a *National Geographic History* article

My boss, the sixth **earl** of Carnarvon, died in September of last
year. As I am not a young man, I had retired as the **butler** of
Highclere Castle, but when young Master Henry asked me to help
him make a **record** of everything of value, how could I refuse?
Of course, I should call young Master Henry "Lord Carnarvon" now
that his father has **passed**, but I've known him since he was a
small boy, so he will always be "Young Master Henry" to me.

We had just finished **cataloging** the last of the **objects**, when the
young earl said that he was glad we were finally done. "Yes," I said.
"Except, of course, for the Egyptian stuff."

◀ **Highclere Castle,
Hampshire,
United Kingdom**

earl a British nobleman
butler chief servant
passed died
cataloging making a list of

"Egyptian stuff? What Egyptian stuff?!" asked young Master Henry, clearly surprised.

I led him to a **passageway** between two of the lower rooms, the doors to which had always stayed locked. There was even heavy furniture placed in front of them to **deter** people from trying to enter. Inside the doors were two secret **panels**. I opened the panels, and Lord Carnarvon reached his arm inside. His face was full of surprise as he removed tins containing the treasures. It had never occurred to me that he did not know about the objects his father had placed here so long ago.

Secret ▶
passageway
in library

---

passageway corridor
deter stop
panels decorative coverings
   for a wall

▶ **Before You Continue**

1. **Fact/Opinion** Which sentence on this page states an opinion? How can you tell?
2. **Main Idea** What will be the main idea of this selection? Why do you think so?

I could hardly **contain** my excitement when Henry—pardon me— when Lord Carnarvon decided that these precious **objects** would be put on display. They will continue to be kept safe here at Highclere Castle as part of an Egyptian **exhibition** for visitors to admire.

However, that's not what I want to share with you today.

When Lord Carnarvon found the treasures, he discovered, in my opinion, something even more **fascinating**—a diary. It was written by his aunt, the Lady Evelyn, who was with her father, the fifth earl, when he discovered Tutankhamun's **tomb** in 1922. **Henry had discovered history.**

▲ **An Egyptian Exhibition in the cellar of Highclere Castle**

contain keep inside

exhibition a display of something important or beautiful

fascinating very interesting

tomb a large vault where the dead are buried

Henry had discovered history. He found something that was very important.

1st October, 1919

I have been so bored here at Highclere. England is such a **dreary** place, and the young men who have come back from **the war** have no interest in parties or dancing. Of course, there was an initial sense of **euphoria** when the war ended, but now the joy has faded.

So it was with much excitement that I received my father's **telegram** from Egypt. Finally, I am to be allowed to visit him and assist on his **archaeological dig**! I am going in one month, but I would leave tomorrow if I could!

▲ **A page from Lady Evelyn's diary**

◀ **Archaeological dig of the tomb of Tutankhamun, Valley of the Kings, Egypt**

dreary dull, bleak

the war World War I, which lasted from 1914 to 1918

euphoria extreme happiness

telegram message

archaeological dig a site being explored for ancient artifacts

▶ **Before You Continue**

1. **Ask Questions** If you could ask Lady Evelyn a question, what would you ask?

2. **Draw Conclusions** How did Lady Evelyn feel about England after World War I?

10th January, 1920

*I have now been here with my father and the archaeologist Howard Carter throughout the winter. My father is getting **frustrated**. He said we won't find anything here—everything has already been **plundered** by grave robbers. But Carter is sure there is an **ancient** tomb **close at hand**. He showed us pictures of **objects** found in this area that bore the name "Tutankhamun," the Egyptian boy King who was only nineteen when he died. Carter has made a map of the **site** showing where he thinks the tomb is.*

My father says his patience is running out, as is his money. Soon, we will return to Highclere, as digs only take place in the autumn and winter when the weather is cooler.

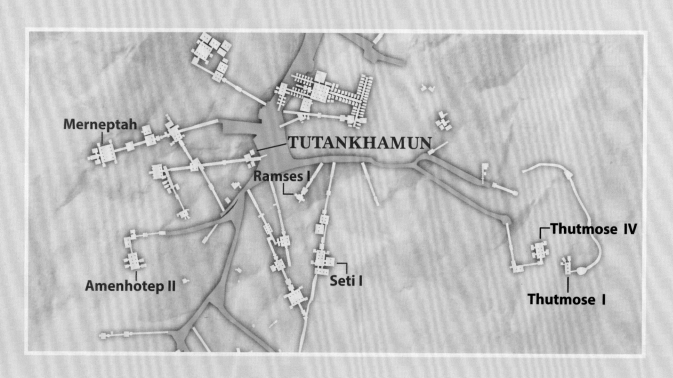

▲ A recreation of Carter's map showing the
tombs of pharoahs found in the Valley of
the Kings

frustrated discouraged
plundered stolen
close at hand nearby

5th November, 1922

Today, after several long, **tedious** months at Highclere, my father has finally received a telegram from Carter! He said he has made a wonderful discovery in the Valley of the Kings. My father is to travel to Egypt immediately, and I am to **accompany** him! I can't imagine what we are about to see.

I hope they can wait for us to arrive.

25th November, 1922

We have finally arrived in Egypt! It's late, and we can't go to the dig until tomorrow. I am so **eager** to see Carter's discovery—a staircase leading to a door. What awaits behind that door, I can **scarcely** imagine.

My Good Lord Carnarvon,

At last I have made a wonderful discovery in the Valley.
A magnificent tomb with seals intact.
Re-covered same for your arrival.

Congratulations!

▲ The unbroken seal on King Tutankhamun's tomb

tedious boring
accompany go with
eager anxious, curious
scarcely barely

▶ **Before You Continue**

1. **Draw Conclusions** Look at the map on page 258 and think about what you've learned so far. Why do you think Carter was sure there was an important tomb in this area?

2. **Main Idea** Why did Carter send a telegram to Lord Carnarvon?

26th November, 1922

As Carter himself said, today was "the day of days, the most wonderful I have ever lived through!"

We arrived at the dig **at first light**, and the staircase was uncovered. This was all that Carter had seen so far, as he wanted to wait for my father before exploring further. He had covered up the staircase after first finding it to prevent it from being discovered by thieves.

The sense of wonder as the staircase was uncovered was as amazing for me as it had been for Carter. He had already seen the door at the end of the staircase, but not the **hieroglyphics** written on them. Imagine our excitement when Carter spelled them out—T-u-t-a-n-K-h-a-m-u-n.

▲ **Entrance to King Tutankhamun's tomb**

▲ **Howard Carter and Lord Carnarvon at the opening of King Tutankhamun's tomb**

at first light early in the morning
hieroglyphics ancient Egyptian writing and symbols

We couldn't wait to see what was behind the door. Carter made a hole to look inside, and for what seemed like **an eternity**, he had his eye pressed to the hole. My father asked him whether he could see anything. "Yes," he replied. "Wonderful things. Wonderful things!"

Finally, my father could bear it no longer. "Let me have a look!" he said. He **gasped** with delight at what he saw. There were paintings of strange animals, statues, and gold everywhere!

The tomb had kept Tutankhamun's treasures safe for more than 3,000 years. Now, it was our responsibility to ensure they were continued to be kept safe. But we also knew, we had to share our discovery with the world.

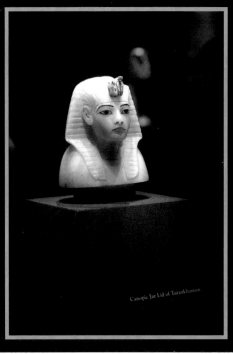

◄ **Treasures found in the tomb**

an eternity a very long time
gasped took a sharp breath.

▶ Before You Continue

1. **Summarize** What did Carter and Carnarvon find behind the door at the end of the staircase?

2. **Make Inferences** Why were Carter and Carnarvon so excited by their discovery?

15th January, 1923

I have not written in this diary for so long, as the treasures of the **antechamber** have held all my attention. We opened the door properly and found that this was not a burial chamber but a room where only <u>some</u> of the King's possessions were kept. Although it appeared to have been partly **looted** in ancient times, there were still many **objects** of value and interest. We found life-size figures, chariots, a **throne** decorated with gold and jewels—in fact, nearly everything was gold! Even a bed!

We have recorded all the items we found and left just two statues guarding another door to what we think is the burial chamber. Now we have to carefully work on opening this door. Who knows what other treasures may be behind it?

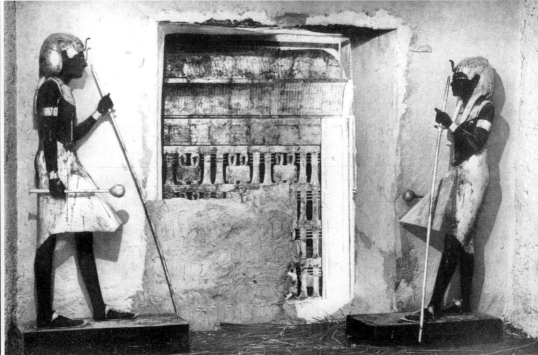

▲ **One of the two life-size statues that stood on each side of the entrance to Tutankhamun's burial chamber for 3,000 years.**

antechamber the room before the main tomb
looted robbed
throne a special chair for a king or queen

16th February, 1923

I think this may have been the best day of my entire life! We finally opened the door to the **burial chamber**. As I am the smallest, I was the one to squeeze in first. Carter's assistant tried, but he couldn't fit inside the small opening at all! He was terribly disappointed.

This room has only one thing inside—a **shrine**. Carter says that inside, we shall find the mummy of Tutankhamun. I suppose some women would find this kind of thing terrifying, but I am <u>not</u> one of those women.

Some are saying the tomb is **cursed**, but they are just silly, **superstitious** people. Tutankhamun died more than 3,000 years ago. We have nothing to fear from him. I just can't wait for the next few days to see what the shrine contains.

burial chamber room where the king was buried

shrine sacred relic

cursed under an evil spell

superstitious having an illogical belief in things unlikely to be true, such as a curse or magic

▶ **Before You Continue**

1. **Fact/Opinion** Carter says the mummy of Tutankhamun should be inside the shrine. Is this a fact or an opinion? Explain.

2. **Sequence** Think about the events leading up to the discovery of the tomb. Describe them in your own words.

26th February, 1923

The reality of the burial chamber was something I could not have imagined, even in my dreams. There were actually three shrines—each inside another. And inside these were a number of gold **sarcophagi**. In the very last one lay the **mummy** of Tutankhamun. He was wearing a golden mask, which was traditional for the Kings of Egypt. It was so **elaborate** and beautiful. It was nearly impossible to **comprehend** that for thousands of years, all of this had lain undiscovered.

We have also discovered another room, which has even more precious treasure in it.

▲ **Tutankhamun's golden death mask**

▲ **Statue on a casket at a Tutankhamun exhibition**

sarcophagi decorated stone coffins
mummy a preserved dead body
elaborate detailed and complicated
comprehend understand

6th April, 1923

My heart is **broken**. Father has died! The doctors said he had blood poisoning from an **infected** mosquito bite, but the **press** is blaming the curse. They say anyone who disturbed the tomb will die. The newspapers are reporting **ridiculous** things. They say that all the lights in Cairo went out at the moment of my father's death, but a blackout is hardly a new occurrence. They are even reporting that my father's old dog, Suzie, died back at Highclere at the very same moment. Rubbish!

I don't believe in curses. My father has never had good health, and he was already 57. For me, this expedition has now come to a **bitter** end.

My heart is broken. I'm very sad.
infected contaminated
press newspapers
ridiculous absurd, crazy
blackout loss of electrical power
bitter sad

▶ **Before You Continue**

1. **Draw Conclusions** Which events made people believe the tomb was cursed? Explain.
2. **Details** Why do you think Lady Evelyn writes that she doesn't believe in curses?

The rest of the story I know only too well. Lady Evelyn came back to Highclere Castle and left Carter to work alone. He knew how important his work was. He carefully recorded all the contents of the tomb. There were more than 5,000 items— it took him *ten years* to complete the **record**!

Carter was **astounded** by many of the things he found, especially all the gold. Tutankhamun's coffin was made of solid gold. His burial mask alone was made with 10 kilograms of gold! There was gold jewelery, golden statues, and even toys and games made of gold.

Around half of the **objects** discovered in the tomb were kept in Egypt by the Egyptian government. The rest were brought back to England.

Gilded wooden statue from the Pharaoh's tomb in Thebes, Egypt ▶

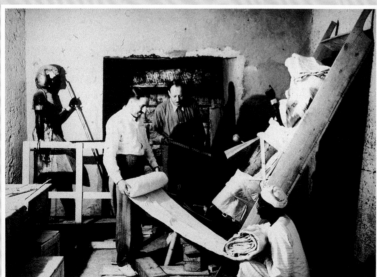

▲ **Howard and a colleague working in the Valley of the Kings**

astounded very surprised

The fifth earl never imagined how fascinated people across the world would be about his and Carter's discoveries. Everyone **was intrigued**.

Life in England after the war was hard, and **landowners** had to pay a lot of **taxes**. The sixth earl had many financial difficulties, so, in 1926, he sold many of the artifacts from the tomb to museums, such as the Metropolitan Museum of Art in New York. The rest of the items, of course, he secretly kept here at Highclere. I am not sure why he locked them away, but I am glad they have once again been found and have finally been put on display for everyone to enjoy. ❖

▲ **Tutankhamen's coffin displayed at the Egyptian Museum in Cairo, Egypt**

was intrigued wanted to know about it
landowners rich people who own property
taxes money paid to the government

▶ **Before You Continue**

1. **Summarize** What happened to all of the **objects** discovered in the tomb?
2. **Analyze** Why do you think the fifth earl hid the artifacts at Highclere?

Think and Respond

Key Words	
ancient	principle
civilization	project
courage	record
empire	risk
object	site
official	

Talk About It

1. What did you learn about Tutankhamun's tomb in this piece of **historical fiction**? Give two facts.

> One fact about Tutankhamun's tomb is _____.
> Another fact is _____.

2. After reading about Lady Evelyn, Lord Carnarvon, and Howard Carter, how do you feel about these people? Why? Explain and **justify** your ideas to a partner.

> I think Lady Evelyn was _____, because _____.

3. Do you think Lord Carnarvon and Howard Carter made the right decision to enter the tomb? Why or why not? Use facts from the story to support your opinion.

Write About It

In your opinion, how did Lady Evelyn show **courage**? Write a paragraph to explain. Include a topic sentence, other sentences that give details, and a conclusion. Use **Key Words**.

> Lady Evelyn showed courage by _____.

Fact and Opinion

Make a fact-and-opinion chart for "Tutankhamun's Treasures."
List examples from the text. Dates are often clues to facts. Words
like *think* and *believe* are clues to opinions. So are words like
wonderful.

Fact-and-Opinion Chart

Facts	Opinions
Ancient Egyptian artifacts were found at Highclere Castle.	England's such a dreary place.
List statements of fact here.	**List statements of opinion here.**

Now use your fact-and-opinion chart as you
analyze "Tutankhamun's Treasures" with a
partner. How could you check that the facts
are true? Use **Key Words** as you talk about
the text.

One fact is _____ .
I could check
by _____ .

Fluency

Practice reading with phrasing. Rate your reading.

Talk Together

Choose a photo of one of the artifacts in "Tutankhamun's
Treasures." Explain why the **object** was worth finding and
showing to the world. Use **Key Words** as you talk about
the object.

Homographs

Homographs are words that are spelled the same but have different meanings. They might be different parts of speech. You often say the words differently, too. You can use context to figure out the correct meaning.

Compare these examples.

The runner set a new speed record. 	The singer gets ready to record a new song. 
Meaning: the best performance written down	**Meaning:** to put information in writing or in another form

Try It Together

Read the paragraph. Then answer the questions.

Carter picked up the <u>object</u> and examined it. He labeled it and put it in a box. Lord Carnarvon changed the label. Carter did not <u>object</u>, even though he believed Lord Carnarvon was wrong.

1. What does <u>object</u> mean in the first sentence?

   A something you can hold

   B a museum

   C to agree

   D to disagree

2. What does <u>object</u> mean in the fourth sentence?

   A something you can hold

   B a museum

   C to agree

   D to disagree

Making Connections Read this story about a woman who saves something very old.

Genre A **historical narrative** tells a story about a real event that happened in the past. The event may follow the plot of a story.

SAVING THE WORLD'S OLDEST LIBRARY

BY ELOISE VIVANCO

Aziza couldn't wait to see the library at the University of al-Qarawiyyin. She had grown up very close to the school, the world's oldest university. And it was founded by a woman!

Aziza was an **accomplished** architect, and, just like Fatima al-Fihri, the founder of the university, she was Muslim. She felt a **flutter of** excitement in her stomach as she walked into the **ancient** building that **housed** the library for the first time.

accomplished highly skilled
flutter of nervous
housed provided space for

▶ **Before You Continue**
1. **Point of View** Is this narrative written in first or third person? How do you know?
2. **Make Inferences** How does Aziza feel about the library? How can you tell?

As she stepped through the **ancient** doors, Aziza couldn't believe her eyes! She looked up to see long cracks in the ceiling. The rooms were damp, and the conditions for storing delicate manuscripts were very poor. Aziza noticed a strange smell, which she later learned was from backed-up water in blocked drains.

The library was **deteriorating**, and with it, all the **precious** ancient documents inside. Aziza thought about how sad Fatima al-Fihri would be to see what had become of her library.

deteriorating falling apart
precious valuable

Aziza had long known about Fatima al-Fihri. She was the daughter of a rich immigrant from al-Qarawiyyin, or *Tunisia*, as it is known today. Al-Fihri was a devout Muslim and a scholar whose family had moved to Fez in Morocco. When her father died, she **inherited** a lot of money. She wanted to use her money to build a place for people in her community to study, learn, and worship.

inherited received

▶ **Before You Continue**

1. **Clarify** What did Fatima want to spend her inheritance on?
2. **Make Inferences** Why do you think Fatima made this decision? What kind of person do you think Fatima was?

Fatima had a university built in Fez and named it after the place she was born—*al-Qarawiyyin*. It was a place of learning for many important poets, philosophers, historians, and economists.

Aziza was born in Fez near the **ancient** university. However, the school had been closed to the public for many years. Only scholars could use it, and even then, only with special permission. As a well-known architect in her native country, Aziza was asked by the **Ministry of Culture** to **assess** the library. She dreamed of making it a place that would serve the whole community once again, as Fatima had **envisaged**. But **restoring** it would be a challenging and expensive **project**.

Ministry of Culture a government organization responsible for spreading culture and history

assess evaluate

envisaged imagined

restoring rebuilding

When Aziza's phone rang a few months later, she **couldn't believe her ears**. The Moroccan Minister of Culture wanted Aziza's **architectural firm** to **renovate** the library. Aziza was so excited that she danced around her desk, the phone still in her hand. She had never imagined that she would be awarded the **contract**, as many people still thought architecture was "a man's job." Fortunately, the Minister of Culture knew better. She was also a woman.

couldn't believe her ears was happily surprised

architectural firm company that designs and constructs buildings

renovate change and improve

contract written agreement to do the job

▶ **Before You Continue**

1. **Draw Conclusions** What kind of person do you think Aziza is?
2. **Explain** Why was Aziza surprised to be awarded the contract?

Renovating the library was an **enormous project** with many challenges to overcome. At first, Aziza felt **overwhelmed**. She discovered so many unexpected problems, it was as though the building was **mocking** her. But little-by-little, step-by-step, she was able to move forward with the renovation.

Aziza made sure to respect the **ancient** building's original architecture and materials, but she still needed to make it **functional** for modern students to use. Sadly, though, some things were impossible to restore and had to be completely replaced.

enormous huge
overwhelmed defeated
mocking making fun of
functional easy to use

The library of al-Qarawiyyin opened to the public once again in 2016. Aziza's **project** was a great success!

Fatima al-Fihri would have been proud of Aziza. She had made the **ancient** library functional again for the people of the city of Fez and restored an important part of their history and their culture. ❖

▶ **Before You Continue**

1. **Summarize** What made Aziza's renovation so successful?

2. **Figurative Language** Why does the author say that the building was "mocking" Aziza?

Respond and Extend

Key Words

ancient	principle
civilization	project
courage	record
empire	risk
official	site
object	

Compare Features

Compare different features of a literary text and an informational text. Work with a partner to complete the comparison chart.

Comparison Chart

	"Tutankhamun's Treasures"	"Saving the World's Oldest Library"
genre	historical fiction	
real or fiction?	real facts with some elements of fiction	
text features	photographs	
point of view		
author's purpose		
how you know the purpose		

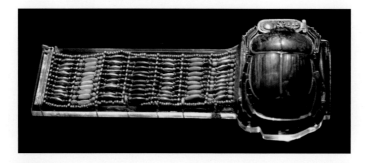

Talk Together

Imagine that you are the authors. Explain why you wanted to write each of these texts. Use **Key Words** as you describe what's worth protecting and sharing with the world.

Future Tense

There are two ways to show the **future tense**.

Grammar Rules Future Tense	
• Use the helping verb **will** along with a **main verb**.	The museum **will display** the ancient artifacts next month.
• Use **am going to**, **are going to**, or **is going to** before a **main verb**.	I **am going to visit** the exhibition. The government **is going to build** a museum. The archaeologists **are going to examine** the objects.

Read Future Tense

Read these sentences about the library of al-Qarawiyyin. Find two examples of the future tense. Identify the main verb in each example.

> When visitors come to the library of al-Qarawiyyin, they will see all the old books in good condition. The library is going to preserve the ancient books.

Write Future Tense

What do you think will happen to the library in the future? Write a paragraph to explain. Use the future tense.

Write as a Reader

Write a Literary Response ✏

Write a response to a story or an article in this unit. Then discuss it with others in your class.

Study a Model

In a literary response, you give your opinion, or personal feelings, about a story or article. You support your opinion with reasons and details.

"Saving the World's Oldest Library"

by Eloise Vivanco
Reviewed by Rajit Shah

Rajit begins with a short summary of the literature.

"Saving the World's Oldest Library" is the true story of Aziza, who worked hard to renovate the oldest library in the world and save the ancient books housed there. **I liked this account because of the information it gives about the difficulties Aziza had, but more details would have made it even better**.

He clearly states his **opinion**.

He gives **reasons** that support his opinion.

Before I read the account, I did not think of books as treasures that should be shared with the whole community. To Aziza, though, it was important that the entire community would be able to share the treasures of the library.

This account **made me think about all the ideas and information that books contain**. What would happen if they all disappeared? I suddenly understood why Aziza thought the library was worth saving.

He uses details from the story to develop ideas.

Prewrite

1. **Choose a Topic** With a partner, review and talk about the literature in this unit. Choose a story or article to write about.

Language Frames	
Tell Your Ideas	**Respond to Ideas**
• I think this story was _____ because _____ .	• What are your reasons for saying _____ ?
• My favorite part of this story was _____ .	• I disagree with you about _____ because _____ .
• Some things I didn't like were _____ .	• What do you mean by _____ ?

2. **Gather Information** What reasons will you give to support your opinion? Reread the literature. Look for details that will help you explain your reasons.

3. **Get Organized** Use a T-Chart to help you organize your thoughts.

T-Chart

What I Liked	What I Didn't Like
The line "Aziza discovered so many unexpected problems, it was as if the building was mocking her."	Not enough details about exactly what Aziza did to restore the library
How Aziza renovated the library, but preserved many of its original features	There wasn't much information about Fatima al-Fihri, the woman who originally built the university.

Draft

Use your chart to write your draft. State your opinion and reasons clearly. Use details from the selection to develop your ideas.

Revise

1. **Read, Retell, Respond** Read your draft aloud to a partner. Your partner listens and then restates your ideas. Then talk about ways to improve your writing.

Language Frames	
Retell	**Make Suggestions**
• Your opinion about the story was _____ .	• I don't understand why you said _____ . Could you explain it differently?
• Your main reasons for your opinion were _____ .	• You didn't include many details from the story. Maybe you could add _____ .
• Some details you used to develop your ideas were _____ .	

2. **Make Changes** Think about your draft and your partner's suggestions. Then use the revision marks to make your changes.

   • Did you state your opinion clearly? If not, try rewording it.

   > because of the information it gives about the difficulties Aziza had, but more details would have made it even better.
   >
   > I liked this account, ~~but it could have been better.~~

   • Use details from the selection to develop your ideas.

   > it was very important that all the community would be able to share the treasures of the library.
   >
   > To Aziza, ~~though, the library was very important.~~

Edit and Proofread

Work with a partner to edit and proofread your literary response. Pay special attention to irregular verbs. Use revision marks to show your changes.

Present

On Your Own Make a final copy of your literary response. Post it on a class blog, or share it with someone who has read the same selection.

Presentation Tips	
If you are the speaker...	**If you are the listener...**
Speak clearly. Pause slightly before sentences and phrases from the literature.	Be ready to summarize the writer's response to the literature.
Be ready to respond to questions about your opinion and reasons.	Think about whether the writer's opinion is supported by details.

In a Group Form a Reader's Circle to discuss the selections you read. Be sure to share both positive and negative opinions. You can also share your opinions in an online discussion group.

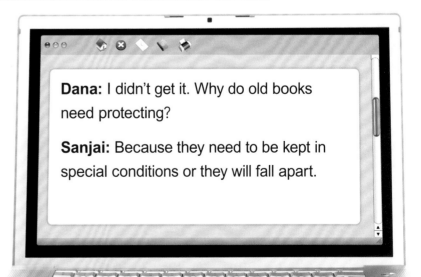

Dana: I didn't get it. Why do old books need protecting?

Sanjai: Because they need to be kept in special conditions or they will fall apart.

? BIG Question

What's worth protecting?

Talk Together

In this unit, you found lots of answers to the **Big Question**. Now make a concept map to discuss the **Big Question** with the class.

Concept Map

records of our history

things that are worth protecting

Write a Persuasive Essay

Choose one thing that you think is worth protecting. Write a persuasive essay about it. Include details to support your ideas.

Share Your Ideas

Choose one of these ways to share your ideas about the **Big Question**.

Write It!

Write a Letter

What social causes do you care about? What organizations would you like to help by volunteering? Write a letter to an organization to learn more about what they do. Include all of the parts of a letter.

Do It!

Make an Ad

Design an ad that asks people to support a cause. Share your ad with the class. Talk about how the words and pictures make the meaning clear.

The Oak Street Soup Kitchen needs your support!

Talk About It!

Share a Superhero Fantasy

Imagine that you are a superhero. Tell a partner what you would do as a superhero to protect something important.

> I would protect all the animals in the ocean!

Do It!

Have a Debate

Talk with classmates about an issue that you think is important to the lives of people today. Then have a debate about it. Discuss different ways to solve the issue.

Picture Dictionary

The definitions are for the words introduced in this book.

Parts of an Entry

The **entry** shows how the word is spelled.

The **picture** helps you understand more about the meaning of the word.

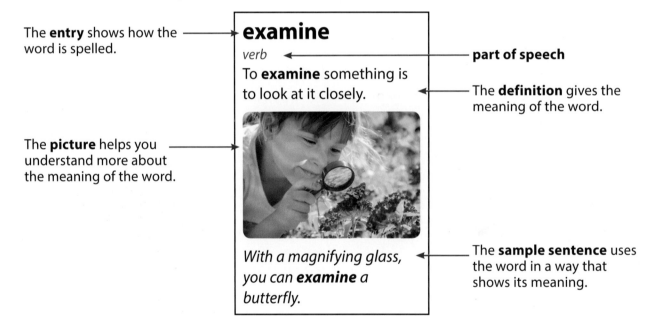

examine

verb

To **examine** something is to look at it closely.

*With a magnifying glass, you can **examine** a butterfly.*

part of speech

The **definition** gives the meaning of the word.

The **sample sentence** uses the word in a way that shows its meaning.

A

accelerate
verb

When something **accelerates** it moves faster.

*A racecar **accelerates** to the finish line.*

adventure
noun

An **adventure** is an exciting experience.

*Early explorers had many **adventures**.*

ancient
adjective

When something is **ancient** it is very old or it happened in the past.

*There are **ancient** buildings all around the world.*

archaeologist
noun

An **archaeologist** is someone who studies old buildings and civilizations.

***Archaeologists** discover new information about ancient cultures.*

artifact
noun

An **artifact** is something that a human made long ago, such as a tool or a weapon.

***Artifacts** such as these arrowheads were used for hunting.*

astronaut
noun

An **astronaut** is someone who travels in space.

***Astronauts** wear special equipment so they can breathe in space.*

average
noun

An **average** is an amount that is usual for a group.

*Bears have an **average** of two cubs.*

*The **average** daytime temperature in a desert is 100°F.*

a b c d e f g h i j k l m n o p q r s t u v w x y z

balance
noun

When something is in **balance**, it is steady.

*If the girl keeps her **balance**, she will not fall.*

capacity
noun

The **capacity** of an object is the most it can hold.

*This glass has a **capacity** of half a pint.*

chart
noun

A **chart** shows information with numbers, pictures, words, and symbols.

*This **chart** is on a computer screen.*

civilization
noun

A **civilization** is an organized society of people.

*There have been many advanced **civilizations** around the world.*

coastal
adjective

Coastal areas are sections of land next to an ocean.

*Large waves often crash into **coastal** areas.*

colony
noun

A **colony** is a region that another country controls.

*These U.S. states were once **colonies** of Great Britain.*

compass
noun

A **compass** is a tool with a magnet that can show you which direction is north.

***Compasses** help sailors know where to go.*

competition
noun

A **competition** is a contest.

*The runners are in **competition** to win the race.*

constant
noun

Something that never changes is a **constant**.

*The number of days in a week is a **constant**.*

contain
verb

To **contain** something is to hold it inside.

*This jar **contains** many coins.*

control
verb

To **control** something is to be in charge of it.

*The driver **controls** where the car goes.*

courage
noun

If you have **courage**, you are brave.

*It takes **courage** to do challenging things.*

currency
noun

Currency is the type of money that is used in an area.

*The dollar is the **currency** in the United States.*

D

decompose
verb

Something **decomposes** when it breaks down. Living things decompose after they die.

*A fallen tree will soon **decompose**.*

discovery
noun

When you find things, you make a **discovery**.

*Her **discovery** is a new germ.*

distance
noun

Distance is the amount of space between two things.

*Today, we can fly a long **distance** very quickly.*

E

empire
noun

An **empire** is a group of countries under one ruler.

*As the Roman **Empire** spread, so did the Latin language.*

a b **c** **d** **e** f g h i j k l m n o p q r s t u v w x y z

a b c d e f g h i j k l m n o p q r s t u v w x y z

environment

noun

An **environment** is the area where something lives.

*Plants grow well in a sunny **environment**.*

*Wet **environments**, such as rain forests, are also rich in plant life.*

examine

verb

To **examine** something is to look at it closely.

*With a magnifying glass, you can **examine** a butterfly.*

experiment

noun

An **experiment** is a test that people do to find out how things work.

*Her **experiment** on plant growth won first prize.*

exploration

noun

An **exploration** is a search.

*Astronauts learn about space from their **exploration**.*

G

galleon

noun

A **galleon** is a large sailing ship that was used hundreds of years ago.

*In the 17th century, people would sail **galleons** all around the world.*

H

habitat

noun

A **habitat** is a place where an organism can live and flourish.

*Some snakes live in a hot, desert **habitat**.*

height

noun

Height is the measurement of how tall someone or something is.

*These girls are about the same **height**.*

heritage

noun

Your **heritage** is the traditions, ideas, and language that come from your ancestors.

*Playing a traditional instrument is part of his Indonesian **heritage**.*

---

hero

noun

A **hero** is a person admired by others for being brave.

*When the firefighter rescued the child, everyone said he was a **hero**.*

humid

adjective

It is **humid** when there is a lot of moisture in the air.

*A hot and **humid** greenhouse is good for plants.*

---

interpret

verb

To **interpret** something is to tell what you think it means.

*Can you **interpret** these road signs?*

introduce

verb

When people **introduce** themselves, they meet for the first time.

*A handshake is a friendly way to **introduce** yourself.*

---

invade

verb

To **invade** something is to take it over without permission.

*Sometimes people **invade** natural habitats.*

---

investigate

verb

When you **investigate** something, you find out about it.

*The boy **investigates** the cave.*

a b c d e f g h i j k l m n o p q r s t u v w x y z

291

launch

verb

When you **launch** something, you send it up into the air.

*This rocket was **launched** into space.*

legend

noun

A **legend** explains symbols on a map.

*This **legend** shows blue lines as rivers.*

limit

verb

To **limit** something is to stop it after a set amount of time.

*Many parents **limit** TV viewing.*

measure

verb

When you **measure** something, you find out its size, weight, or amount.

*The girl is using a ruler to **measure** her cat.*

*The scale **measures** the weight of the orange.*

merchant

noun

A **merchant** is someone who buys or sells items.

*People buy fish from this **merchant**.*

migration

noun

During a **migration**, people or animals move from one place to another.

*These birds fly south in their yearly **migration**.*

mission

noun

A **mission** is a job with a goal.

*Their **mission** is to rescue people after an earthquake.*

mold
noun
Mold is a fungus that grows on old food.

*This bread has a lot of **mold** on it.*

motion
noun
Motion is movement.

*A racecar's **motion** is very fast!*

motive
noun
A **motive** is a reason for doing something.

*One **motive** for studying is to get good grades.*

native
adjective
When living things are **native** to an area, they live and grow there naturally.

*In many desert regions, the cactus is a **native** plant.*

navigation
noun
Navigation is the process of figuring out how to get somewhere.

*With careful **navigation** the boat can pass through the icebergs safely.*

*Sailors use a compass for **navigation**.*

object
noun
An **object** is something that isn't alive that you can touch and see.

clock

remote control

ball glove

*These are all **objects**.*

official
adjective
When something is **official**, it's approved.

*This **official** seal is from the president's office.*

a b c d e f g h i j k l **m** **n** **o** p q r s t u v w x y z

a
b
c
d
e
f
g
h
i
j
k
l
m
n
o
p
q
r
s
t
u
v
w
x
y
z

orbit

verb

In space, something **orbits** when it moves around a sun, a moon, or a planet in a predictable path.

*The planets **orbit** around the sun.*

Ⓟ

planet

noun

A **planet** is a large body that orbits around the sun or another star.

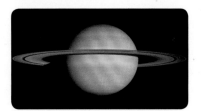

*Saturn is one of the **planets** in our solar system.*

population

noun

The **population** is the number of living things that are in an area.

*China has a very large **population** of people.*

port

noun

A **port** is a safe place where boats can dock.

*The boats stay in the **port**.*

preserve

verb

To **preserve** something is to keep it safe from harm.

*Use photo albums to **preserve** old pictures.*

president

noun

A **president** is an elected leader of a country.

*George Washington was the first **president** of the United States.*

principle

noun

A **principle** is a rule or law.

*Some U.S.A. laws are based on the **principles** of freedom.*

project

noun

A **project** is a job or activity.

*Building a skyscraper is a huge **project**.*

*Sustainable agriculture is a worthwhile **project**.*

protect
verb

You **protect** something when you guard it against harm.

*Seat belts help to **protect** people in cars.*

Ⓡ

rate
noun

The **rate** of an action is its speed.

*Turtles move at a slow **rate**.*

record
noun

A **record** of something is the facts about what happened.

clay tablet ▷

*Because many ancient people wrote down information, we have a **record** of their lives.*

resistance
noun

Resistance is a slowing force.

*Deep snow creates **resistance** when you walk in it.*

responsible
adjective

A person who is **responsible** is in charge.

*This dad is **responsible** for his son.*

risk
noun

Risk is the possibility of harm.

*Wearing a helmet lowers your **risk** when you ride a bike.*

a b c d e f g h i j k l m n o **p** q **r** s t u v w x y z

a
b
c
d
e
f
g
h
i
j
k
l
m
n
o
p
q
r
s
t
u
v
w
x
y
z

rotation
noun

The **rotation** of something is how it turns around its axis.

*A globe shows the **rotation** of Earth.*

route
noun

A **route** is a path to go someplace.

*Do you take the shortest **route** to school?*

Ⓢ

scale
noun

A **scale** gives size comparisons.

1"=1 mile

*The **scale** of this map shows that 1 inch is equal to 1 mile.*

service
noun

When something is of **service**, it is useful.

*A cart is of **service** when you move heavy boxes.*

site
noun

A **site** is a special place where something happened.

*People study archeological **sites** to learn about ancient cultures.*

solve
verb

To **solve** a problem means to figure it out.

*When you **solve** a puzzle, it's done.*

species

noun

A **species** is a group of living things that are very similar and can have offspring.

*Cats and dogs are different **species**.*

speed

noun

Speed is how fast something is going.

*A racecar travels at a very high **speed**.*

spore

noun

Spores are small, seed-like structures that are made by plants that don't reproduce using flowers.

*A fern reproduces by releasing **spores**.*

spread

verb

To **spread** is to cover a wider area.

*Flies can **spread** diseases.*

technology

noun

Technology is the use of science to solve problems.

*Doctors rely on **technology**.*

threatened

verb

Something is **threatened** when it is in danger.

*Because of habitat destruction, many rainforest animals are **threatened**.*

trade

verb

To **trade** is to exchange one thing for another.

*The friends **trade** toys.*

treasure

noun

A **treasure** is a collection of jewels, money, or other valuable items.

*Gold coins are the **treasure** in this chest.*

*The girl finds a **treasure** while panning for gold.*

a b c d e f g h i j k l m n o p q r **s** **t** u v w x y z

a
b
c
d
e
f
g
h
i
j
k
l
m
n
o
p
q
r
s
t
u
v
w
x
y
z

value

verb

To **value** something is to care about it.

*Many people **value** saving money.*

volunteer

noun

A **volunteer** is someone who helps out with a task without being paid.

*This **volunteer** is giving food to people who need it.*

Index

Index of Authors

Index of Illustrators

Text and Illustrator Credits

Unit Five

Scholastic Press: From "The Fungus that Ate My School" by Arthur Dorros, illustrated by David Catrow. Scholastic Inc./Scholastic Press. Text copyright © 2000 by Arthur Dorros, illustrations copyright © 2000 by David Catrow. Used by permission.

Exploratorium: Excerpt from "Mold Terrarium" from www.exploratorium.edu, September 9, 2009. Copyright © 1998 by Exploratorium. Reprinted by permission.

Peachtree Publishers: First published in the United States under the title "Aliens from Earth: When Animals and Plants Invade Other Ecosystems" by Mary Batten, illustrated by Beverly J. Doyle. Text Copyright © 2003, 2016 by Mary Batten. Illustrations Copyright © 2003, 2016 by Beverly J. Doyle. Published by arrangement with Peachtree Publishers.

Island Observations: Christy Finlayson, National Geographic grantee.

Unit Six

New England Pirate Museum: Excerpt from "Make a Treasure Map" by the New England Pirate Museum from www.piratemuseum.com, March 5, 2009.

Texas Historical Commission: "La Belle Shipwreck" by the Texas Historical Commission, Texas Archeological Research Laboratory, University of Texas, Austin. Original article from the Texas Beyond History website www.texasbeyondhistory.net, March 2009.

Unit Seven

Albert Whitman & Company: "What's Faster than a Speeding Cheetah?" by Robert E. Wells. Copyright © 1997 by Robert E. Wells. Used by permission of Albert Whitman & Company.

Penguin Random House: Illustrations by Jerry Pinkney, copyright © 2008 by Jerry Pinkney; and entire text from "The Moon Over Star" by Dianna Hutts Aston, text copyright © 2008 by Dianna Hutts Aston. Used by permission of Sheldon Fogelman Agency and Dial Books for Young Readers, an imprint of Penguin Young Readers Group, a division of Penguin Random House LLC. All rights reserved. Any third party use of this material, outside of this publication, is prohibited. Interested parties must apply directly to Penguin Random House LLC for permission.

Unit Eight

Clarion Books: Abridged from "Buffalo Music" by Tracey E. Fern. Copyright © 2008 by Tracey E. Fern. Used by permission of Clarion Books, an imprint of Houghton Mifflin Harcourt Publishing Company. All rights reserved.

Photographic Credits

Cover © Bachir Moukarzel. iii (tl) Solvin Zank/ Minden Pictures. (tr) Ethan Daniels/Stocktrek Images/Getty Images. (bl) NASA. (br) Andrew Milligan - PA Images/Getty Images. 2–3 Solvin Zank/Minden Pictures. 3 Liz Garza Williams/ Hampton-Brown/National Geographic School Publishing. 5 (bg) SunnyMeansSixteen/ Shutterstock.com. (l) Tom Hoenig/Getty Images. (r) Tom Hoenig/Getty Images. (inset) Paul Zahl/ National Geographic Image Collection. 7 (tl) shippee/Shutterstock.com. (tc) Dennis Jacobsen / Dreamstime.com. (tr) Lobsang Studio/Stockbyte/ Getty Images. (bl) Leander Baerenz/Photodisc/ Getty Images. (bc) Steve Allen/The Image Bank/ Getty Images. 21 Arthur Dorros. 25 Mark Thiessen/Hampton-Brown/National Geographic School Publishing. 26 Mark Thiessen/Hampton-Brown/National Geographic School Publishing. 27 Mark Thiessen/Hampton-Brown/National Geographic School Publishing. 28 Mark Thiessen/ Hampton-Brown/National GeographicSchool Publishing. 29 (t) Foodcollection/mediabakery. com. (b) Scimat/Science Source. 30 (tl, tc) Mark Thiessen/Hampton-Brown/National Geographic School Publishing. (bl) Take Photo/Shutterstock. com. 31 Henri Koskinen/Shutterstock.com. 37 (tl) Alistair Berg/Getty Images. (tc) Image Source/ Photodisc/Getty Images. (tr) g-stockstudio/ Shutterstock.com. (bl) Burazin/Photographer's Choice/Getty Images. (bc) John Elk III/Lonely Planet Images/Getty Images. 58 Kristen Elsby/Moment/Getty Images. 60 (tl) Dr. Christy Leppanen. (tr) Kevin Schafer/ Photolibrary/Getty Images. (cl, cr) Morales/AGE Fotostock. (b) Chris Newbert/Minden Pictures/ Getty Images. 61 (l, r) W. Perry Conway/Corbis/ Getty Images. 62 Dr. Christy Leppanen. 63 Dr. Christy Leppanen. 70 (t) Solvin Zank/Minden Pictures. (b) Paulius Beinaravicius/Shutterstock. com. 71 (bl) Ingram Publishing/Getty Images. (br) American Images Inc/Getty Images. 72–73 Ethan Daniels/Stocktrek Images/Getty Images. 73 Liz Garza Williams/Hampton-Brown/National Geographic School Publishing. 75 (t) Candela Foto Art/ Kreuziger/Getty Images. (bl) Classic Image/ Alamy Stock Photo. (br) George Doyle/Stockbyte/ Getty Images. 77 (tl) Comstock/Stockbyte/Getty Images. (tc) tomas del amo/Alamy Stock Photo. (tr) UniversalImagesGroup/Getty Images. (bl) Johnny Adolphson/Shutterstock.com. 78 Bill Bachman/Alamy Stock Photo. 79 Phil Martin/ PhotoEdit. 83 Lutsenko_Oleksandr/Shutterstock. com. 97 Courtesy of Steve Trussel. 101 scol22/ iStock/Getty Images. 102 (tl) P Maxwell Photography/Shutterstock.com. (tcl) Ruslan Ivantsov/Shutterstock.com. (tc) Hugh Threlfall/ Alamy Stock Photo. (tcr) Daboost | Dreamstime. com. (tr) Roman Sahaidachnyi | Dreamstime.com. (bl) scol22/iStock/Getty Images. (br) Stephen Rees/ Shutterstock.com. 103 scol22/iStock/Getty Images. 107 (t) Roger Morris/National Geographic Image Collection. (c) Marcos Brindicci/REUTERS. (b) Ira Block/National Geographic Image Collection. 109 (tl) North Wind Picture Archives/Alamy Stock Photo. (tc) Tatevosian Yana/Shutterstock.com. (tr) Comstock/Getty Images. (bl) David Buffington/ Blend Images/Getty Images. (bc) Image Source/ Stockbyte/Getty Images. 114 National Maritime Museum, London/The Image Works. 115 History and Art Collection/Alamy Stock Photo. 116 (t) National Maritime Museum, London/The Image Works. (b) Paul Popper/Popperfoto/Getty Images. 119 Bruce Dale/National Geographic Image Collection. 126 (bl) Pam Susemiehl/Getty Images, (br) JASON EDWARDS/National Geographic Image Collection. 126–127 Andrew Bain/Getty Images. 131 (bg, c) Expedition of Robert Cavelier de La Salle (1643–87) in Louisiana in 1684, 1844 (oil on canvas)/Gudin, Jean Antoine Theodore (1802–80)/ Château de Versailles, France/Bridgeman Images. (b) MPI/Getty Images. 132 (b) GRANGER. (t) Expedition of Robert Cavelier de La Salle (1643– 87) in Louisiana in 1684, 1844 (oil on canvas)/ Gudin, Jean Antoine Theodore (1802–80)/Château de Versailles, France/Bridgeman Images. 132–133 Expedition of Robert Cavelier de La Salle (1643– 87) in Louisiana in 1684, 1844 (oil on canvas)/ Gudin, Jean Antoine Theodore (1802–80)/Château de Versailles, France/Bridgeman Images. 133 (t) Expedition of Robert Cavelier de La Salle (1643– 87) in Louisiana in 1684, 1844 (oil on canvas)/ Gudin, Jean Antoine Theodore (1802–80)/Château de Versailles, France/Bridgeman Images. (b) Dolph Briscoe Center for American History, The University of Texas at Austin. 134 (t) Expedition of Robert Cavelier de La Salle (1643–87) in Louisiana in 1684, 1844 (oil on canvas)/Gudin, Jean Antoine Theodore (1802–80)/Château de Versailles, France/ Bridgeman Images. (b) Charles Shaw/Texas Historical Commission. 134–135 Expedition of Robert Cavelier de La Salle (1643–87) in Louisiana in 1684, 1844 (oil on canvas)/Gudin, Jean Antoine Theodore (1802–80)/Château de Versailles, France/ Bridgeman Images. 135 (t, b) Texas Historical Commission. 142 Ethan Daniels/Stocktrek Images/ Getty Images. 143 (t) Michael Newman/PhotoEdit. (b) mateu/iStock/Getty Images. 144–145 NASA. 145 Liz Garza Williams/Hampton-Brown/National Geographic School Publishing. 147 (tl) Jonathan Ferrey/Getty Images. (tr) arenacreative/iStock/ Getty Images. (bl) FatCamera/Getty Images. (br) John W. McDonough/Getty Images. 148 (l) Stocktrek/Photodisc/Getty Images. (r) Digital Vision/Getty Images. 149 (tl) Daniel J. Cox/Oxford Scientific/Getty Images. (tc) Comstock/Stockbyte/ Getty Images. (tr) Zoltan Tarlacz/Shutterstock.com. (bl) boris64/iStock/Getty Images. (bc) travellinglight/ iStock/Getty Images. 152–153 Andy Rouse/The Image Bank/Getty Images. 156 Allkindza/Getty Images. 157 Time Life Pictures/Getty Images. 158 Tony Hallas/Getty Images. 162 Adrian Baras/ Shutterstock.com. 163 John Greim/Getty Images. 166 danabeth555/Getty Images. 167 (bg) Digital Vision./Getty Images. (cr) Withan Tor/Shutterstock. com. 168 (bg) Be Good/Shutterstock.com. (b) Stockbyte/Getty Images. 169 Be Good/ Shutterstock.com. 170 Be Good/Shutterstock.com. 171 (bg) Be Good/Shutterstock.com. (bl) Universal Images Group North America LLC/Alamy Stock Photo. 175 (t) stockphoto mania/Shutterstock.com. (tr) viafilms/iStock/Getty Images. (bl) Howard Shooter/Dorling Kindersley/Getty Images. (br) Fuse/Getty Images. 177 (tl) Evgeniia Bezuglova/Shutterstock.com. (tc) alexsl/Getty Images. (tr) greenland/Shutterstock.com. (bl) XiXinXing/Shutterstock.com. (bc) Jonatan Fernstrom/Cultura/Getty Images. 178 (l) Hulton Archive/Getty Images. (r) Universal Images Group North America LLC/Alamy Stock Photo. 179 SolidMaks/Shutterstock.com. 187 Everett Collection Historical/Alamy Stock Photo. 192 DonSmith/Alamy Stock Photo. 195 AP Images/ Dake Kang. 198 Rolls Press/Popperfoto/Getty Images. 199 Bettmann/Getty Images. 200 (t) NASA/Getty Images. (b) NASA Johnson Space Center. 201 (t, b) NASA/Getty Images. 207 FatCamera/Getty Images. 208 NASA. 209 (bl) Withan Tor/Shutterstock.com. (bcl) Thomas Northcut/Getty Images. (bcr) Sam Armstrong/ Getty Images. (br) yulicon/Shutterstock.com. 210–211 Andrew Milligan - PA Images/Getty Images. 211 Liz Garza Williams/Hampton-Brown/ National Geographic School Publishing. 213 (tl) Ariel Skelley/Blend Images/Getty Images. (tr) Jeff Schultz/Design Pics/Getty Images. (bl) Michelle D. Bridwell/PhotoEdit. (br) National Archives and Records Administration. 215 (tl) AP Images/Niigata Nippo via Kyodo News. (tc) Tetra Images/Alamy Stock Photo. (tr) Ted Foxx/Alamy Stock Photo. (bl, bc) Image Source/Getty Images. 220 Philip Scalia/Alamy Stock Photo. 224 J Need/Shutterstock. com. 233 Tracey Fern. 234 Larry Gerbrandt/Getty Images. 237 Larry Gerbrandt/Getty Images. 238 (t) Marilyn Angel Wynn/Corbis Documentary/Getty Images, (c) Indian Encampment, 1892 (gouache on paper)/Farny, Henry Francois (1847–1916)/ CHRISTIES IMAGES/Private Collection/Bridgeman Images, (b) Marilyn Angel Wynn/Nativestock/ Getty Images. 238–239 Medioimages/Photodisc/ Getty Images 239 (t) GRANGER — All rights reserved. 240 (t) Omikron/Science Source. 240 (tr) Union Pacific Railroad poster advertising the first transcontinental railroad across the USA, 1869 (colour litho), American School, (19th century)/ Private Collection/Peter Newark American Pictures/The Bridgeman Art Library. (bl, br) GRANGER — All rights reserved. 240–241 GRANGER — All rights reserved. 241 (t) Paul Fearn/Alamy Stock Photo. (b) Len Collection/ Alamy Stock Photo. 242 Library of Congress/Corbis Historical/Getty Images. 242–243 Anh Luu/

Acknowledgments

The Authors and Publisher would like to thank the following reviewers and teaching professionals for their valuable feedback during the development of the series.

Literature Reviewers

Carmen Agra Deedy, Grace Lin, Jonda C. McNair, Anastasia Suen

Global Reviewers

USA:

James M. Cleere, Teacher, Donald McKay School, Boston, MA; **Judy H. Cole,** ESL Teacher, Southwestern Randolph Middle School, Asheboro, NC; **Aimee R. Finley,** Bilingual Teacher, C. A. Tatum Jr. Elementary School, Dallas, TX; **Laura Hook,** Elementary ESOL Resource Teacher, Faulkner Ridge, Catonsville, MD; **Michelle Navarro,** Teacher on Special Assignment, Orange Unified School District, Orange, CA; **Theresa Proctor-Reece,** ELL Teacher, Windy River Elementary School, Boardman, OR; **Kathy Walcott,** Spanish Immersion Specialist, Rockford Public Schools, Rockford, MI; **Michelle Williams,** ELL & Migrant Programs Director, West Ottawa Public Schools, Holland, MI

Asia:

Mohan Aiyer, School Principal, Brainworks International School, Yangon; **Andrew Chuang,** Weige Primary School, Taipei; **Sherefa Dickson,** Head Teacher, SMIC, Beijing; **Ms Hien,** IP Manager, IPS Vietnam, Ho Chi Minh; **Christine Huang,** Principal, The International Bilingual School at the Hsinchu Science Park (IBSH), Hsinchu; **Julie Hwang,** Academic Consultant, Seoul; **David Kwok,** CEO, Englit Enterprise, Guangzhou; **Emily Li,** Teaching Assistant, SMIC, Beijing; **Warren Martin,** English Teacher, Houhai English, Beijing; **Bongse Memba,** Academic Coordinator, SMIC, Beijing; **Hoai Minh Nguyen,** Wellspring International Bilingual School, Ho Chi Minh; **Mark Robertson,** Elementary School Principal, Yangon Academy, Yangon; **Daphne Tseng,** American Eagle Institute, Hsinchu; **Amanda Xu,** Director of Teaching and Research, Englit Enterprise, Guangzhou; **Alice Yamamoto,** ALT, PL Gakuen Elementary School, Osaka; **Yan Yang,** Director of Research Development, Houhai English, Beijing

Middle East:

Lisa Olsen, Teacher, GEMS World Academy, Dubai, United Arab Emirates; **Erin Witthoft,** Curriculum Coordinator, Universal American School, Kuwait

Latin America:

Federico Brull, Academic Director, Cambridge School of Monterrey, Mexico; **Elizabeth Caballero,** English Coordinator, Ramiro Kolbe Campus Otay, Mexico; **Renata Callipo,** Teacher, CEI Romualdo, Brazil; **Lilia Huerta,** General Supervisor, Ramiro Kolbe Campus Presidentes, Mexico; **Rosalba Millán,** English Coordinator Primary, Instituto Cenca, Mexico; **Ann Marie Moreira,** Academic Consultant, Brazil; **Raúl Rivera,** English Coordinator, Ramiro Kolbe Campus Santa Fe, Mexico; **Leonardo Xavier,** Teacher, CEI Romualdo, Brazil

The Publisher gratefully acknowledges the contributions of the following National Geographic Explorers to our program and planet:

Christy Finlayson and Constance Adams